THE LEGACY OF
FOR ABORIGINAI

Education, Oppression, and Emancipation

BERNARD SCHISSEL & TERRY WOTHERSPOON

OXFORD
UNIVERSITY PRESS

OXFORD
UNIVERSITY PRESS

70 Wynford Drive, Don Mills, Ontario M3C 1J9
www.oupcanada.com

Oxford University Press is a department of the University of Oxford.
It furthers the University's objective of excellence in research, scholarship,
and education by publishing worldwide in

Oxford New York

Auckland Cape Town Dar es Salaam Hong Kong Karachi
Kuala Lumpur Madrid Melbourne Mexico City Nairobi
New Delhi Shanghai Taipei Toronto

with offices in
Argentina Austria Brazil Chile Czech Republic France Greece
Guatemala Hungary Italy Japan Poland Portugal Singapore
South Korea Switzerland Thailand Turkey Ukraine Vietnam

Oxford is a trade mark of Oxford University Press
in the UK and in certain other countries

Published in Canada
by Oxford University Press

National Library of Canada Cataloguing in Publication Data

Schissel, Bernard, 1950-
The legacy of school for Aboriginal people: education, oppression,
and emancipation / Bernard Schissel and Terry Wotherspoon.

Includes bibliographical references and index.

ISBN-10: 0-19-541664-3   ISBN-13: 978-0-19-541664-0

1. Native youth–Education–Canada–Social aspects. 2. Indians of North America–
Canada–Residential schools. 3. Native youth–Education–Saskatchewan–Case studies.
I. Wotherspoon, Terry II. Title.

E96.2.S34 2002   306.43'08997071   C2002-903096-X

Cover design: Joan Demspsey

6 7 8 - 09 08
This book is printed on permanent (acid-free) paper ∞.
Printed in Canada

CONTENTS

DEDICATION TO RACHEL

ACKNOWLEDGEMENTS

The experiences at the heart of this book emerged from a study entitled 'An Investigation into Indian and Métis Student Life Experience in Saskatchewan Schools' that the authors conducted for Saskatchewan Education as part of an initiative through the Aboriginal Education Research Network sponsored and funded by that province's Department of Education. The authors gratefully acknowledge the encouragement and funding support of Saskatchewan Education, and in particular the tireless efforts and commitment of Gillian McCreary and Jan Runnells to ensure the project was undertaken and completed successfully.

The authors also acknowledge the funding support of grants from the Social Sciences and Humanities Research Council of Canada, the SSHRCC-funded New Approaches to Lifelong Learning, the Strategic Research Network in Education and Training, and the Council of Ministers of Education Canada Pan-Canadian Education Research Agenda. We thank, as well, the University of Saskatchewan's Office of Research Services for funding support for the manuscript. We are grateful for the dedication and sensitivity demonstrated by Roseanne Morphy and Tina Nicotine, who conducted the fieldwork and background preparation for the study. We have learned much and gained a stronger sense of humanity from our graduate students Darlene Lanceley and Helen Quewezance, who keep the struggle alive. Jason Doherty has provided extensive and timely assistance as deadlines approached for completion of the manuscript. We are fortunate to work in a setting—the Department of Sociology at the University of Saskatchewan—that is rich in intellectual stimulation and collegial support, as well as to benefit from the insights and collegiality of people in other departments and institutions. As always, our family members have encouraged us and provided the inspiration for our ideas and commitments.

The completion of this book has benefited significantly from the professional work and encouragement of staff at Oxford University Press. Acquisitions editor Megan Mueller, in particular, has provided strong guidance and support for the project from its inception to manuscript completion. We also acknowledge the suggestions and recommendations of the anonymous reviewers of the proposal and manuscript, and Richard and Laurna Tallman for their editorial skills.

Lastly, we wish to thank the First Nations students who generously shared their thoughts and experiences. Their insights and suggestions have provided the framework for this book and, despite their youth, they have shown guidance and wisdom.

PREFACE

Educational success is widely acknowledged to be an essential tool for social and economic success. Our expectations about what education systems should offer all citizens rise in conjunction with the expanding realm of knowledge, social skills, and technical competencies that people require to negotiate global challenges and new economies.

Schooling itself—at least to the extent that it is an educational enterprise rather than simply a bureaucratic agency—is transformative in nature. Its concern is not merely to transmit formal lessons and bestow credentials, but to develop personalities and identities: to alter the way that people understand themselves, other people, the social and natural worlds, and their relationships with those worlds. These broadly defined educational relations are critical elements of our humanity and sociability in the sense that human beings have the unique capacity to reflect and act upon the world. Schooling, therefore, is educative in a positive or progressive way to the extent that it may enable us to nurture and advance our human, social capacities.

This book is a contribution to ongoing efforts to understand and address the educational aspirations and realities of Aboriginal people in Canada. It is comprised of a summary of literature we consider relevant to our subject, a view of past efforts to provide education to Aboriginals, and a preliminary research study that we believe has profound implications for Aboriginal learning and should provide a springboard for further research into this important branch of Canadian education. To enhance the utility of the book in the college classroom, the first two chapters mark important terms and concepts in boldface type and Questions for Critical Thought accompany each chapter. In addition to the literature reviewed in Chapter 2 there is an extensive Bibliography with suggestions for further reading and an annotated list of relevant Internet Web sites.

Aboriginal people's expectations are high that education carries with it the means to improve their life prospects, and they are clearly aware that schooling as they have known it must be retooled to enhance the chances that their aspirations can be achieved. Within broad visions of educational improvement, considerable debate about educational possibilities reflects the diversity of people's experiences, dreams, and life conditions. There is a lack of consensus, overall, in regard to the nature of Aboriginal people's place in Canadian society. The federal government appears disinclined to develop a systematic action plan in response to the 1996 Report of the Royal Commission on Aboriginal Peoples and its vision of a renewed relationship based on principles of recognition, respect, sharing, and responsibility. Divided public opinion and political stances create confusion over what 'the problem' is, whose responsibility it is, and how best to address it. In the latter half of 2001, the National Chief of the Assembly of First Nations, Matthew Coon Come, condemned Canada for its institutionalized racism in the course of attempts by the Minister of Indian Affairs to restructure drastically the Indian Act, which regulates the lives of First Nations people and their communities. Meanwhile, even in the absence of a unified pathway, various new initiatives are emerging in response to the needs and desires of Aboriginal people in education and other institutional domains and sectors.

We cannot pretend to comprehend fully, or to speak from the perspective of Aboriginal students, their families, and community members, nor to communicate adequately their pains, frustrations, hopes, and successes associated with schooling and the experiences that they bring with them into schooling. But we have turned our research tools to their educational history and to contemporary Aboriginal children and youth, whose voices are rarely heard or acknowledged in discussions of education policy and related curriculum matters. Aboriginal education is not a new issue. In the studies reported here we have found some of what has gone badly wrong, some of the educational approaches for Aboriginal youth that work well, and some strategies that point the way to better learning opportunities for Aboriginal people within the mainstream educational system.

This book has its origins in several sources related to the authors' research, work, and personal experiences. Both authors have taught and worked with Aboriginal students and community members, including teaching at the high school and university levels and conducting applied research with rural and urban Aboriginal communities. Our conversations and encounters with indigenous students, colleagues, and others have impressed upon us how many of them have struggled with conflicting dimensions associated with being—and being identified as—Aboriginal in institutional settings dominated by non-Aboriginal people. The pains and joys of cumulative experiences have led sometimes to frustration and despair, but also to hopes and efforts to create more promising futures for themselves and their children.

Chapter 1

EDUCATIONAL DREAMS AND DISAPPOINTMENTS

ASPIRATIONS AND EXPERIENCES

• Lots of times the teachers don't understand the situations or they don't understand certain people, they are used to seeing their middle-class kids attending and being good students. I guess if one of those teachers came into this school their head would spin off their shoulders because there are so many different people with different problems and mostly everybody has some problems because most the students are young parents. Eighty per cent of the student population here [at my high school] is considered at risk. (Grade 12 student, First Nations of mixed heritage)

• I would say the white race would have it easier in some places, like this one school that I went to in [a small town] . . . they weren't used to Native culture, and when I first went there in Grade 7 and stayed till Grade 8. When I first got there they were like making fun of me, like where did you set up your tipi and do you ride into town on your horse and stuff like that. (High school student, Poundmaker First Nation)

• I know it's really really important to get my education, my mom has really stressed that and seeing her . . . my mom has been in school all my life too. (Grade 12 student, Dakota Sioux)

• I was having an argument with this one guy, he's of Chinese descent, he says he believes in Jesus Christ. You know, every kid gets into that argument. I wasn't downplaying his beliefs and I wasn't trying to upstage [boast about] mine, but Red Bull, one of Wanuskewin's traditional dancers, came in and as we were walking to the assembly we were still arguing, he was like . . . well, what's your belief then? And there was the smell of sweet grass in the air because they were smudging, and I said, you smell that, that's what I believe in. Then I started to explain to him the fundamentals of burning sweet grass and our beliefs, which was totally a form of educating him, not preaching, you know—there is a huge difference, I hold that dear, you know, respecting each others' cultures and values. (Grade 12 student, Blackfoot, Siksika First Nation)

The voices of Aboriginal youth, as of Canadian youth in general, represent a diversity of experiences, perspectives, and hopes. The above quotations highlight several dimensions of these realities. Schools often are vehicles that point the way to future promise and prospects for the fulfillment of personal and community aspirations. However, schools can also be harsh environments that produce bitterness and failure, or reinforce external social problems like racism, poverty, violence, and victimization. Cultural practices and belief systems associated with Aboriginal heritage are often ignored or undermined in conventional education, but schools can sometimes introduce indigenous students to their roots in ways that evoke powerful responses. In short, formal education, or schooling, is critically important for its ability to provide the kinds of experiences, knowledge, skills, and credentials required for success in contemporary Aboriginal communities and Canadian society; but it is also implicated in the processes that contribute to failure and marginalization among large segments of the Aboriginal population.

Numerous studies and reports in recent years have drawn attention to the dark side of education, implicating schools in processes that have badly damaged or even destroyed the lives and futures of many Aboriginal people and their communities (see, especially, Royal Commission on Aboriginal Peoples, 1996b: 333 ff.; 1996c: 433 ff.). The immediate and long-term impacts of physical, sexual, and psychological abuses against Aboriginal students in residential schools are now the subject of several public apologies by the agencies and officials responsible for those schools, a series of lawsuits by residential school survivors, and a statement of reconciliation and healing strategy adopted by the federal government. While today's schools may often be more inviting, or at least less hostile, environments, Aboriginal students continue to be less likely than average to complete school or, if they do, to continue beyond high school into further education. In the course of extensive consultations with community groups, Aboriginal organizations, and submissions from other sources, the Royal Commission on Aboriginal Peoples (1993: 19) identified education as 'the single most important issue facing Aboriginal people'.

The need to ensure adequate educational opportunities and meaningful inclusion in educational processes has become increasingly critical in what is commonly referred to as the knowledge or learning society. Formal education has become a requirement for entry into jobs and participation in other social sites. Education also has importance over and above socio-economic advancement. It is important for shaping self-esteem, for raising awareness and sensitivity related to one's own and other cultures, and for contributing to the development of an active citizenry in accordance with the demands of a democratic society. Canadians, in general and increasingly, are attaining higher levels of education, gaining more education than their parents, continuing their educational careers for longer periods of time, and pursuing education to upgrade their credentials throughout much of their lives. While this is true across nearly all social groups and categories of people, those who are best-situated and who have more education tend to be the ones most likely to take advantage of continuing educational opportunities (de Brouker and Lavallée, 1998; Guppy and Davies, 1998; Livingstone, 1999). In other words, for those who begin life in situations where their educational horizons are limited, there is a high probability that the education gap will perpetuate itself, or become wider, over time even if they do eventually persist in their schooling. Low rates of educational attainment, in turn, are related to reduced life prospects and higher chances of experiencing poverty, unemployment, and other life difficulties. Conversely, many commentators have emphasized that, for Aboriginal people even more than for the general population, improved educational attainment is positively associated with the likelihood of integration into the labour market, improved employment prospects, increased earning potential, and reduced dependence on government transfer payments (Hull, 2000: 108–9; Jankowski and Moazzami, 1995: 109–10; Santiago, 1997: 32).

Despite the pressing need for improved educational access and completion rates among Aboriginal people, there are many highly qualified Aboriginal people, growing numbers of whom are firmly committed to improving both their own credentials and the educational circumstances in the communities they come from or work in. Education has long been a focal point in the struggles by Aboriginal people to regain control over their lives and circumstances, signified formally in 1972 with the adoption by the National Indian Brotherhood (a forerunner to the Assembly of First Nations) of a policy of 'Indian control of Indian education'. Since that time, significant steps have been taken, by First Nations and other

Aboriginal agencies, as well as by non-Aboriginal bodies, to ensure opportunities for meaningful participation and outcomes by Aboriginal learners in varied educational settings.

THE PURPOSE OF THIS STUDY

Aboriginal education is a diverse world of aspirations, experiences, disappointments, and hopes. The study of that world can be undertaken from a variety of perspectives. The purpose of this book is to explore Aboriginal education more fully and to examine the political, socio-economic, cultural, and personal pathways related to it. As such, this book is intended to provide a platform for further exploration and study. The following questions need to be answered. They are posed as guides to the discussion of these issues, even if it is not possible to offer definitive answers at this stage.

- What are the current dimensions of educational participation and outcomes among Aboriginal populations in Canada?
- What historical and contemporary social factors account for these trends?
- What factors do Aboriginal students identify as the strengths and limitations of their schooling?
- How relevant is schooling, according to the perceptions of Aboriginal students, to their out-of-school experiences and aspirations?
- What are the prospects for Aboriginal education in Canada?

In addressing these questions, we rely on a variety of sources and applications for information. Our analysis focuses on trends and issues relevant to many Aboriginal people across Canada. The last part of this chapter points to the need to understand the diversity that is characteristic of the Aboriginal population. Many of the issues and examples we discuss represent First Nations, though we also discuss matters relevant to various categories of Aboriginal identity or ancestry, or to Aboriginal people living in specific kinds of social circumstances or regions. In Chapter 4, for example, we illustrate our analysis through extensive reference to research oriented to the experiences of First Nations and Métis children and youth attending schools in Saskatchewan. We draw from a combination of historical and contemporary experiences to provide a context within which we can gain a more complete understanding of these educational circumstances.

Our focus is directed, in particular, to the interactions among human agents and social structures, which make up the processes by which individual aspirations and experiences become translated into divergent pathways and unequal outcomes. Each person encounters his or her schooling through a composite of personal characteristics or capabilities and opportunities based on his or her own family and community backgrounds, which in turn are heavily influenced by a complex array of social, economic, historical, cultural, and political forces in the larger community. Individuals bear considerable responsibility for their own choices and destinies, but none of these is independent of powerful circumstances that often lie beyond the capacity of the individual to manage or control. To illustrate: a repeated finding from Canadian and international research is that while children and youth typically hold high educational aspirations, many fall short of their goals or modify them as their life journeys take unanticipated turns or detours (Anisef et al., 2000: 50 ff.). Moreover, although it is possible for individuals from any given social background to achieve educational success (or failure), there are relatively stable patterns, reflecting such social characteristics as gender, race, class, family support, and region, that typify achievement and contribute to the likelihood that some people are more likely than others to realize their educational ambitions and to convert their training and credentials into enhanced prospects in other areas of their lives. To examine how these processes operate, it is essential to gain an understanding, in both historical and contemporary terms, of how educational practices operate in conjunction with other social spheres or structures, such as labour markets, community conditions, policy frameworks, and race relations.

ABORIGINAL PEOPLE AND THEIR EDUCATION

Why is a study of the education of Aboriginal people significant? It may appear to some observers that this subject does not warrant special attention since Aboriginal people are presumed to have the same rights and chances for schooling as any other Canadians. Moreover, there are numerous examples of educational successes and failures, and of special educational initiatives, among many minority groups. Contemporary emphasis on the learning society forces all individuals to look ahead, whatever the evidence of past injustices. Aboriginal people do share with many other groups a diverse range of educational options, experiences, and ambitions. Therefore, we must not become so overly preoccupied with past disappointments and failures that we obscure important success stories and the opportunities that do exist.

Nonetheless, there are several significant reasons for paying special attention to the nature of and prospects for education among Canada's Aboriginal population. First, the persistence of an **education gap** between Aboriginal people and the general population is of increasing concern to Aboriginal communities and organizations as well as to federal, provincial, and territorial government agencies, employers, community groups, and educators (see, e.g., Federation of Saskatchewan Indian Nations, 1997; Royal Commission on Aboriginal Peoples, 1996c).

Second, there is a troubling **equity disparity** between Aboriginal educational opportunities and those of other Canadians. The Canadian ethos of equity and fairness that is central to democratic societies and processes and outcomes declares that no group of people should be held in positions of continuing disadvantage.

Third, the **expansion of self-government** means that it is essential that Aboriginal people have meaningful opportunities to broaden their education in order to fulfill expectations for their own personal and community development. There are increasing demands for a substantial pool of trained, qualified personnel to fill positions in service and employment sectors operated by both Aboriginal and non-Aboriginal agencies or governments.

Fourth, an understanding of education for Aboriginal people draws attention to much **uniquely Aboriginal experience** deserving of preservation and perpetuation, as well as to factors that are shared with various groups.

Fifth, sensitivity to **indigenous Aboriginal knowledge**, as well as to diverse forms and systems of Aboriginal education—whether traditional or emerging through new initiatives and self-government developments—can offer tremendous insights into a more general understanding of educational practices and developments.

As the quotations that begin this chapter reveal, Aboriginal education experiences involve many facets besides disadvantage and failure in conventional systems. Many Aboriginal people have achieved remarkable success, in part through formal education. In addition, they have longstanding bases of knowledge and knowledge systems of their own.

It is important, as well, to recognize that education for Canada's

Aboriginal people takes place in a variety of institutional and informal settings that are shaped by complex historical developments and given shape by personal experiences, in ways that reflect the diverse nature of the Aboriginal population. The term 'Aboriginal' can be misleading, and is often rejected by many of the people to whom it is commonly applied, especially when it is used merely as a label or when it presumes a degree of homogeneity that undermines a person's or a group's unique cultural traditions, identities, and life circumstances. It becomes a meaningful concept when it comprehends the diversity of people who have some common cultural backgrounds or identities as indigenous people. The Aboriginal population is marked by considerable social differentiation, which operates at two interrelated levels. Aboriginal people are distinguished from other Canadians by particular legal statuses and historical, social, and cultural experiences, but like any social group their circumstances are also marked by internal differences and inequalities (Wotherspoon, 2003).

SOCIAL DIFFERENTIATION AND ABORIGINAL PEOPLE

Aboriginal people constitute a relatively small proportion (about 4.5 per cent) of the total Canadian population, but their presence, history, contributions, and future prospects are profoundly significant not only for themselves, but for their relations with the larger society. The Aboriginal, or indigenous, population includes all people whose ancestry derives from **the first inhabitants of the land**, whose established roots, social systems, and economic and land-use patterns predate European contact by several centuries. Aboriginal people, in general, are distinct from other groups in a number of ways, reflecting shared aspects of their heritage and their unique legal and political status as first peoples. There is now legislative and constitutional recognition of Aboriginal rights and Aboriginal status, designated in turn by the identification of three main categories: **Indians or First Nations**, the **Métis**, and the **Inuit** (Cairns, 2000; Royal Commission on Aboriginal Peoples, 1996a, 1996b).

This recognition accounts for one of the dimensions of differentiation and diversity within the Aboriginal population. Legal categories take into account, in part, cultural differences, but they also may be **socially constructed**, i.e., develop from definitions and historical practices imposed by governments. One way these legally imposed differences are expressed is in the difficulties now associated with efforts to identify the dimensions of the Aboriginal population. The Department of Indian and Northern Affairs Canada (2000: 4) estimates a total Aboriginal population of 1,399,300. Just under half of this population is classified as status Indians (persons registered under the Indian Act), constituted by 28.5 per cent of the total population living on-reserve and 20.8 per cent living off-reserve; 15.6 per cent of the total are classified as Métis, 4.5 per cent as Inuit, and 30.6 per cent are non-status Indians (those not registered under the Indian Act). The term 'First Nations' refers to designated communities or bands (by 2000, the Department of Indian and Northern Affairs recognized 609 First Nations, while the Assembly of First Nations recognized over 630), and their membership, where membership is determined in accordance with terms set out under the Indian Act, broadly parallels those persons registered under the Act but also allows for some First Nations to control their own membership (Assembly of First Nations, 2000).

Adding to this complexity of designation, different rights and entitlements are attached to whether or not persons have **legal status,** whether or not a person is eligible and accepted for band membership, whether band members are living on or off a reserve, and whether or not they are members of First Nations that signed treaties or claims agreements with the British Crown or Canadian government. In addition, cultural factors such as ancestry and linguistic groups produce further degrees of differentiation. On the 1996 census, just over 1.1 million people reported Aboriginal ancestry while 799,010 persons indicated their identity as Aboriginal persons, though it is important (1) to recognize that census figures under-report the number of Aboriginal people, and (2) to take into account population growth since that time (Statistics Canada, 1998a: 3). As shown in Table 1.1, which details the number of persons reporting Aboriginal ancestry in the 1996 census, the size and concentration of the Aboriginal population vary across regions. While the largest numbers of Aboriginal people live in Ontario and British Columbia, over 11 per cent of people in Saskatchewan and Manitoba, one in five in the Yukon, and nearly 62 per cent of Northwest Territories residents have Aboriginal ancestry. (In Nunavut, which gained status as a distinct territory in 1999, 84 per cent of the population of about 24,900 were estimated in 1995 to have had some Inuit origins; see Stout, 1997: 14.) A growing majority, now about 55 per cent of the Aboriginal population, live in urban or metropolitan areas, about 30 per cent live on rural reserves, and about 20 per

Table 1.1 Distribution of Aboriginal Population in Canada

	North American Indian	Métis	Inuit	Total Aboriginal Population	Total Population	Aboriginal Population as a % of the Total Population
Canada	867,225	220,740	49,845	1,101,955	28,528,125	3.9
Nfld	14,330	4,560	7,100	24,590	547,155	4.5
PEI	2,125	330	55	2,400	132,855	1.8
NS	24,860	1,405	810	26,795	899,965	3.0
NB	16,040	890	275	17,095	729,630	2.3
Que.	113,000	22,025	9,450	142,385	7,045,080	2.0
Ont.	214,085	31,990	3,025	246,070	10,642,795	2.3
Man.	96,580	48,345	490	138,890	1,100,295	12.6
Sask.	91,445	325,490	390	117,350	976,615	12.0
Alta.	117,465	45,745	1,645	155,650	2,669,195	5.8
BC	157,800	29,610	1,685	184,445	3,689,755	5.0
Yukon	6,060	365	115	6440	30,650	21.0
NWT	13,435	3,060	24,810	39,850	64,125	62.1

Figures may add to more than totals due to multiple responses.

Figures based on ethnic origin responses.

Compiled from Statistics Canada publications 93F0025XDB96002 and 93F0025XDB96001. Based on a 20% sample of the 1996 census.

cent live in other rural (and often isolated or far northern) communities (Statistics Canada, 1998a: 4).

Apart from legal definitions and demographic factors, considerable variations in **socio-economic** and **personal circumstances** prevail within Aboriginal populations. It is crucial to acknowledge the need for fundamental improvement in areas such as housing, living conditions, employment, health care, and education for Aboriginal people in general, but we must also avoid stereotypes that undermine the complexity of real challenges, life prospects, visions, voices, and determinants of success that exist within the population. **Gender differences** are produced and reinforced through the varying challenges, life circumstances, issues, interests, and forms of representation available to Aboriginal men and women as they struggle to gain control over their lives. **Conditions on reserves** vary greatly even within regions, with potential for disparities to widen as a consequence of such factors as the nature and pace of self-government, variable access to human and natural resources, social and economic development initiatives, and political structures. First Nations people living on- and off-reserve often have differential **access to education, occupational and social opportunities**, and **government and community services**, along with social and economic relationships and other options that affect quality of life. These realities point to an awareness that Aboriginal people's experiences and circumstances are shaped in some respects by shared factors that are a consequence of their Aboriginality (such as rights or exclusions that emerge from legal distinctions or policies, broad cultural heritage, or encounters with discrimination and racism), as well as by factors associated with places in society that may be shared with non-Aboriginal groups.

Education is central to these diverse aspirations and circumstances. **Formal education** can open doors to future social opportunities, but it is also affected by, and often reinforces, the social positions and experiences that accompany people into schooling. Schooling is also a critical site of social participation in its own right, affecting a person's orientation to self, to others, and to the world in general. As noted earlier, there have been some significant general improvements in schooling outcomes among Aboriginal people, fostered in part by important developments within education, as well as in conjunction with an overall increase in educational emphasis and attainments among the Canadian population.

Just as there has been a profusion of sites and forms of education associated with the growth of 'the learning society', Aboriginal people have access to diverse educational services. First Nations students now have unprecedented opportunities to attend schools under the jurisdiction of their bands or tribal councils. **Band-operated schools** have experienced steady growth since their introduction in the early 1970s, enrolling about one-third of on-reserve students by the late 1980s and reaching about 60 per cent of the on-reserve student population by the end of the twentieth century (Department of Indian Affairs and Northern Development Canada, 2000: 35). However, the majority of students of Aboriginal ancestry, including registered First Nations students living off-reserve, Métis, and indigenous people without First Nations status, attend **provincial and territorial schools**. Others are in **private schools** or **alternative programs** outside the conventional school system. In addition, Aboriginal people are engaged in numerous **adult and continuing education** programs as well as informal learning endeavours on their own or with others. Further education or training opportunities for Aboriginal people occur through the transmission of **indigenous knowledge and programs guided by Elders**. Nonetheless, many Aboriginal youth remain either in transition or out of any recognized educational program, on a short-term basis or longer.

These trends carry with them mixed implications. It is likely that social and economic opportunities will open up to increasing numbers of Aboriginal people as they gain educational credentials and other competencies. Expanded capabilities will enhance their ability to enter into more meaningful jobs and open doors into other valued social, economic, and political positions, but barriers remain to the fulfillment of the promise associated with educational growth.

The age profile of the Aboriginal population is significant. The **Aboriginal population profile** is on average 10 years younger than the general population. This gap is projected to grow because about one-third of Aboriginal people identified in the 1996 census were children under 15, compared with one-fifth of the total population (Statistics Canada, 1998a: 6). These trends are encouraging insofar as younger people in both populations are better educated than those in older age cohorts, with less-pronounced education gaps between the two populations in the lower age cohorts (Canadian Council on Social Development, 2000: 15–17; Department of Indian Affairs and Northern Development, 2000: 28–9). However, there is also concern that the gaps will grow if improvements in educational participation and attainment rates slow down. Moreover, high concentrations of Aboriginal children and youth live in **rural and remote regions** or experience personal circumstances, such as **homelessness, family breakdown, or periodic migration between communities**, that sometimes leave them poorly served by educational services, facilities, and opportunities.

Analysis of the 1996 census reveals that, among Canadians aged 15–19, about 30 per cent of Aboriginal youth, compared to fewer than 10 per cent of visible minority youth and about 15 per cent of persons in non-racialized groups born in Canada, had not completed high school and were not attending school in the previous year (Canadian Council on Social Development, 2000: 15–16). Moreover, Aboriginal children and youth tend to have much higher than average likelihood of being in categories (such as poverty or living in a lone-parent family) associated with a high risk of not completing school or experiencing later problems in life.

It is important to acknowledge that many persons who are designated 'at-risk' or who do leave high school early do eventually return to school and may experience subsequent educational and social success. Despite this probability, a precarious balance continues, especially for people with the least access to essential resources and social supports, contributing to disproportionate opportunities and gaps among groups later in life. Consideration must be given to why some people or groups are better able than others to achieve their educational aspirations, and to the ways in which education-related outcomes are differentially produced by various social mechanisms, processes, and opportunity structures.

CONCLUSION

We have outlined in this chapter several dimensions associated with both the promise and failure of schooling to enable Aboriginal people to realize their aspirations. We have located schooling in a social, economic, and historical context that has contributed to social differentiation. In their heritage, experiences, and identities Aboriginal people are distinguished in important ways from other Canadians, but the indigenous population itself reflects diverse living conditions, needs, interests, and aims. The relative lack of education among Aboriginal people, in comparison with the general population, remains a critical problem despite some signs that the 'education gap' is closing. There are both qualitative and quantitative dimensions to this concern—getting more education is essential for access to social and economic opportunities, but the kind of education people have and how it relates to their social backgrounds and future orientations are also important.

In subsequent chapters, we explore these issues with particular reference to historical and social factors that have contributed to these educational trends and prospects, and to the perceptions of Aboriginal students about their schooling experiences. Our concern in Chapter 2 is to consider some of the main theories or frameworks that various writers have drawn upon to understand these issues in more depth. Following that, we draw attention to a number of substantive dimensions of schooling and the social context within which education is organized and practised. Chapter 3 explores the nature and legacy of residential schooling, with reference both to how it has undermined educational prospects for substantial proportions of the Aboriginal population in previous generations and to its lasting impact on individual lives and their subsequent engagement (or lack of engagement) in spheres of social life beyond schooling. In Chapter 4, we turn to an assessment of educational practices, exp tions, and aspirations through the eyes and voices of Aboriginal yo four exceptional Saskatchewan schools. These stories enable us to e some of the reasons to be optimistic about the future, and also sensitize us to several factors around which caution or substantial improvements are required. Chapter 5 examines factors that give rise, alternatively, to hope for educational improvement in Aboriginal communities and to concern for the continuing inability of education to achieve desired changes. Finally, Chapter 6 focuses on the future, with a discussion of the social context and policy perspectives within which prospects for viable educational alternatives may be accomplished.

QUESTIONS FOR CRITICAL THOUGHT

1. What are the main consequences and benefits for Aboriginal people posed by Canada's education systems?

2. Who is included in the formal, legal definition of Aboriginal people, and who is excluded? How do these official distinctions affect access to education and other services?

3. The Royal Commission on Aboriginal Peoples identified education as 'the single most important issue facing Aboriginal people'. Discuss why special consideration should be given to this issue. What are the main prospects and challenges education offers for Canada's Aboriginal people?

4. Should governments consider Aboriginal people as a single, unified group when developing future policies? Why or why not? Discuss the implications of this issue for new educational policies and practices.

5. What are the main purposes of formal education? To what extent should educational change be guided by economic forces? What other factors are important in developing education, both in general and with special relevance for Aboriginal people?

RECOMMENDED READING

Assembly of First Nations and National Indian Brotherhood. 1987. *Tradition and Education: Towards a Vision of Our Future.* Ottawa and Summerstown, Ont.: AFN and NIB.

  This report offers a comprehensive summary of First Nations conceptions of education, outlines in detail the meaning and nature of education for First Nations, and provides several case studies to illustrate innovative educational initiatives.

Battiste, Marie, and Jean Barman, eds. 1995. *First Nations Education: The Circle Unfolds.* Vancouver: University of British Columbia Press.

  This volume addresses major challenges and successes on the path to fulfilling the educational aims of Canada's First Nations. Employing the Sacred Circle or medicine wheel as an organizing principle, the book includes chapters on indigenous conceptions of education, teaching and learning issues, school dropouts, curricular innovations, post-secondary and adult education, and relations between schooling and Aboriginal cultural orientations.

Castellano, Marlene Brant, Lynne Davis, and Louise Lahache, eds. 2000. *Aboriginal Education: Fulfilling the Promise.* Vancouver: University of British Columbia Press.

  This edited collection provides a useful overview of major educational problems and developments especially pertinent to issues raised by the Royal Commission on Aboriginal Peoples in its 1996 Report. With contributions from both Aboriginal and non-Aboriginal educators and scholars, the book includes research conducted in conjunction with (but never published by) the Royal Commission, and details policy developments that led to and have followed from the Commission Report. Central areas of concern include Aboriginal languages, educational practice, post-secondary education, and educational policy.

National Indian Brotherhood. 1972. *Indian Control of Indian Education: A Position Paper.* Ottawa: NIB.

This work remains significant as an expression of the educational vision of Canada's First Nations. Written in response to federal government proposals to dismantle the Indian Act, it outlines why Aboriginal people see control over and development of culturally appropriate education as an essential step in assuring their children's futures with a meaningful place in Canadian society.

Royal Commission on Aboriginal Peoples. 1996. *Report of the Royal Commission on Aboriginal Peoples*, vol. 3, *Gathering Strength*. Ottawa: Minister of Supply and Services Canada.

The Royal Commission, established in 1991, conducted extensive public hearings, community site visits, research, and analysis to establish a framework with the aim of restructuring the relationship between Aboriginal people and non-Aboriginal people in Canada. This volume offers a comprehensive overview of and policy vision for education and other key areas of social programming.

CHAPTER 2

ABORIGINAL EDUCATION IN CANADA: ISSUES AND THEORIES

INTRODUCTION

The previous chapter highlighted the importance of formal education in contemporary social life, pointing to discrepancies with respect to schooling that many Aboriginal people face both in comparison with the population as a whole and in relation to their own aspirations. In this chapter, we look at how different analysts or writers who have adopted particular orientations have tried to make sense of these issues. We outline the major theoretical explanations that have been applied to the social and educational developments experienced by Aboriginal people. The chapter concludes with an outline of our own approach, based on an understanding of how individual aspirations and decisions are framed within a complex network of social relationships and structures, policies, and material circumstances.

THEORETICAL APPROACHES TO AN UNDERSTANDING OF ABORIGINAL EDUCATION

As educators, policy-makers, academic researchers, and community members themselves have attempted to make sense of the kinds of problems and issues faced by Aboriginals, they have drawn upon a wide range of analytical frameworks and theories. This section provides examples of different theories that writers of various orientations or perspectives have employed to explain the gap in the educational experiences or outcomes between Aboriginal people and other Canadians.

A **theory** is primarily a tool used to develop a **systematic understanding** or explanation of a given problem or set of phenomena. The intent of any theory is to help us understand why things are as they are and how they have come to be that way. Regardless of what we are trying to explain—whether our concern is with how and why dinosaurs disappeared, or how to make sense of changing weather patterns, or what factors contribute to criminal behaviour, or how social change occurs—we rely on theories to help us organize and make sense of the facts at our disposal, to guide our search for new facts, evidence, or counter-evidence, and to create linkages among the various pieces of information at our disposal. There are usually several different, and often competing, theories about many social and natural phenomena due to the complexity of the issues under consideration, because our knowledge of basic facts and relevant connections is incomplete, or because there logically are alternative frameworks through which the central issues are defined and examined. A theory, then, incorporates assumptions (which may be either implicit or explicit) about what the world is like and how it is organized in order **to link together ideas and empirical data** about what we know about the problems or phenomena we are concerned with.

Various writers have employed various theoretical 'windows' or perspectives on the development of Aboriginal education, drawing attention to diverse factors, assumptions, interpretations, and focal points in educational history and social relationships. Here we summarize some of the main theoretical approaches or perspectives, which we categorize, broadly, as **liberal, cultural, institutional**, and **structural** in emphasis. We conclude with an outline of an approach that we consider to offer the most complete understanding of Aboriginal education. This orientation offers a critical analysis that takes into account the interplay among **social structure, individual agency, and specific material circumstances**. It is this latter theoretical structure that the reader needs to carry forward into the chapters that follow to understand the point of view from which information is presented.

LIBERAL-INDIVIDUALIST APPROACHES

Individualist or **liberal** theories locate the responsibility for success or failure with each **person**, sometimes advocating for economic and policy frameworks that ensure that **individual rights** can be accommodated and made accountable. Accounts or theories of this kind stress that variable rates of educational attainment and achievement are a consequence primarily of differing levels of **capacity, effort, initiative, or skill** among individual learners. Social and policy interventions, as viewed from this perspective, should be restricted to efforts to minimize or remove barriers that prohibit each person from being able to compete on an equitable basis with others for scarce resources. In other words, once it can be assured that Aboriginal people have the same opportunities as other Canadians to attend and participate in school, it is up to individuals and their families to produce results. Consequently, a person with this theoretical position, on being shown data that Aboriginal people have lower than average educational success, is likely to conclude that Aboriginals themselves possess inadequate levels of initiative, capability, or investment in educational processes.

Among supporters of the liberal-individualist theory are those who stress **biological determinants** to explain the racialized stratification of North American education systems and labour markets. This viewpoint has been stimulated by the high profile given to books such as *The Bell Curve* (Herrnstein and Murray, 1994). Other liberal-individualist authors are more concerned about the contributions made by policy and economic frameworks to what they characterize as racially based cycles of segregation and dependency that conspire to undermine individual rights and incentives and restrict Aboriginal people's interactions in the spheres of activity that are required for social success. Thomas Flanagan's assessment that we must turn away from what he calls the 'aboriginal orthodoxy' towards policies that promote Aboriginal people's **assimilation or integration** into market economies and conventional political processes provides a recent example of this kind of approach. Aboriginal people, he argues, will not get ahead until government gets 'out of the way'. Otherwise, they:

> have little sense of real-world trade-offs because everything their governments do for them is paid for by other people. They never have to give up anything in order to get additional programs. If they had to make the same claims that other Canadians routinely make, they would, I predict, take the axe to many of the government programs proliferating luxuriantly in their communities. (Flanagan, 2000: 197–8)

Although the criticism of some dimensions of government programs and of the absence of viable alternatives for self-sufficiency is well-placed, the imagery of well-endowed programs and the lack of sacrifice is certainly contradicted by widespread personal and collective reports of experiences of victimization, deprivation, and lack of government responsiveness to pressing needs among Aboriginal communities. Nonetheless, there is considerable public and political support for these views,

Wallat

expressed most strongly by neo-liberal and conservative political parties, as well as by those members of the public disinclined to approve of 'special status' for Aboriginal people. Such support, though, has tended to diminish or become more ambivalent over time as people become more aware of Aboriginal issues (Ponting, 1998: 284–5).

Liberal and market-based approaches sometimes point to useful critiques of the limitations of present institutional and government structures, but they tend to underplay or fail to acknowledge at all the impact of the deeply rooted **structural inequalities** and continuing barriers to equitable social participation and outcomes. This 'turning of the blind eye' to social inequities is compounded by ideological and analytical stances that suggest that Aboriginal rights are a fiction. There are, however, matters of fact to refute this stance: real legal and institutional frameworks built on the acknowledgement of indigenous rights, historical agreements and relationships, and contemporary agreements and negotiations.

Furthermore, within liberal theory, there is often an affinity between liberal-individualist approaches and **human capital theory,** which highlights the need to invest in knowledge and education in order to enhance economic performance at both individual and societal levels. Human capital theory draws attention away from people's inherent limitations or characteristics in the sense that it acknowledges the need for a social or policy commitment to build upon and broaden existing capacities. This position accepts that there is some justification for expanding the range of education and training services where it is likely that unfulfilled potential for development, that is, the existence of a pool of 'wasted' talent, is detrimental to productivity growth. This theoretical perspective has frequently been applied to the recognition of Aboriginal people as a relatively 'untapped resource' to fuel Canada's emerging labour market needs.

Human capital theory has become especially apparent as the Aboriginal population grows, in marked contrast to the more generally declining birth rates and aging population in the rest of Canada. The disparate birth rates and age structures of the Aboriginal and overall Canadian populations have triggered demands for education systems to ensure that sufficient numbers of Aboriginal people are qualified and prepared to enter into jobs where workers will be required (Canadian Labour Force Development Board, 1994: 66–7; Foot, 1996: 197–8). These trends, within a human capital orientation, are associated with an economic or consumer orientation to education, as illustrated in the following statement from an analysis conducted for the Federation of Saskatchewan Indian Nations (1997: 90):

> The increasing Aboriginal student population will be a customer seeking relevant programs. Educational institutions should be seeking out Aboriginal professionals to meet their future resource requirements. Programs and educational initiatives will have to be relevant, applicable, and sensitive to Aboriginal needs. Although this changing population base will evolve over time, institutions must begin to address the human resource and programming challenges.

A common assumption within liberal and human capital approaches is that when appropriate forms of education and training are widely available, unregulated labour markets will be positioned to absorb the available human capital while an expanding general pool of knowledge and talent will induce further technological development and economic growth. It is fairly easy to accept this kind of analysis, at least at face value, at an intuitive and often an individual level. In the case of Aboriginal people, for instance, the attainment of high levels of educational credentials has a strong impact on reducing or even removing gaps in employment and earnings relative to their non-Aboriginal counterparts (Armstrong et al., 1990: 42; Santiago, 1997).

However, human capital approaches, like other individual-oriented perspectives, remain limited in their ability to explain the persistence of educational inequality and its relationship to economic and labour market inequality (Livingstone, 1999: 169–70). Although educational improvements have created new opportunities for Aboriginal people at both individual and community levels, significant barriers within education systems, job markets, racially based ideologies, and other social sites make it difficult for many of them to realize their educational aspirations and nurture and utilize their talents fully (Royal Commission on Aboriginal Peoples, 1996c: 433 ff.). These inequalities are deeply rooted in material and psychological circumstances that require policy intervention and social action well beyond attention to individual factors.

CULTURAL ORIENTATIONS

An approach that sometimes overlaps with the liberal-individual focus, though often with more empathy for Aboriginal perspectives, incorporates theories based on **cultural factors** or differences. Cultural theories are distinguished by their emphasis on characteristics shared by members of specific populations based on common heritage, identity, or claims. These features, particularly when they are applied to racial minorities such as Aboriginal people, are often highlighted in such a way as to **emphasize differences** from the dominant or mainstream culture. Much early educational analysis focused in this way on those elements of Aboriginal culture—orientations to time and work, collective values, child-raising practices—that are perceived as detriments to their educational performance or success. Whether portrayed negatively or in a more well-intended manner, such emphases often perpetuate stereotypes and lead to explanations of the relative lack of educational success among Aboriginal people as the consequence of deficits or deficiencies in their cultures. Nagler (1975: 32), for instance, takes note of the colonizing impact of previous educational policies but concludes that 'The difficulties that the Native People have had in participating fully in the Canadian educational system stem largely from the fact that they are not ready to integrate culturally with the larger society, and that that society is not receptive to what are considered socially and culturally alien peoples.'

One of the central assumptions employed by earlier educational policy and practice, particularly within the residential school system, was the notion that Aboriginal children would have to be separated from their families and cultures in order to gain full exposure that would allow them to assimilate into Euro-Canadian culture. Besides the obvious flaws in assessments that pose minority cultures as inferior to, or more primitive than, the dominant one, **cultural deficit approaches** are misleading or dangerous in three other major ways—they tend to focus on cultures as phenomena that develop in **isolation** from one another and remain relatively static over time; they assume that the **dominant culture and its standards are neutral or superior** and that success depends on people's ability to assimilate into it; and they fail to acknowledge the **richness and diversity of other cultures.**

More recently, attention has been given to what is sometimes called a '**cultural discontinuity** thesis' that shifts the blame for failure from Aboriginal cultural traditions to the gap between this heritage and the schools and other institutions that represent the dominant society. Conventional educational practices, though officially neutral and oriented to democratic participation and fairness for all participants, are governed by expectations, standards, and procedures that nevertheless reflect the values of the dominant culture and are imposed without regard either for the cultural beliefs and community traditions of minority students or for issues that arise as students attempt to **make a transition** from one cultural framework to another (Chisholm, 1994: 33–4; Douglas, 1994; Gabriel Dumont Institute, 1993: 25). Ryan (1996: 116) summarizes these differences:

> For the most part, Native children continue to attend schools that are structured in ways that differ only marginally from the organizational patterns that were imposed by Europeans. The same hierarchies, divisions of space and time, and systems of accountability continue to pervade modern formal education and to convey a similar level of mistrust and disrespect—and with it a subordinate status—towards Native peoples not only at the classroom level, but also at a community and societal level.

Many writers have posed these relationships in more critical terms, emphasizing the impact of cultural conflict and the **imposition of standards and practices**, by institutions and representatives of the dominant culture, that weaken or destroy the heritage, social relations, and identities of Aboriginal people (Jaine, 1993; Miller, 1996; Royal Commission on Aboriginal Peoples, 1996b: 365 ff.). These institutional approaches emphasize that it is not cultural differences themselves, but rather the ways in which they have been constructed and used by dominant groups, that have led to **devaluation**, **marginalization**, or **destruction** of the knowledge, practices, and relationships essential to Aboriginal societies.

Cultures, viewed this way, are not neutral or benign phenomena that exist and develop either independently from or side by side with one another. Schools and other formally **organized social agencies**, such as criminal justice and social welfare systems, churches, the mass media, and legislatures, are cultural institutions in the sense that they play an active role in defining, transmitting, and shaping what are regarded as legitimate or normal cultural expectations and practices. Even common thinking about culture reflects a **cultural bias** in the sense that we come to emphasize racial or ethnic minorities characterized by cultural traits or forms of 'distinctness' that place them in sharp contrast to a society dominated by white European-based qualities. This domination has become so pervasive that there has been little public sensitivity to 'whiteness' as a form of culture, or to how European cultural referents, in contrast to alternative cultural frameworks, have come to be regarded as normal (Kincheloe, 1998). In fact, as the history of residential schooling, discussed in more detail in the next chapter, illustrates, such **cultural domination** has been the result of both active and indirect sources, through a combination of discriminatory practices, **regulatory frameworks**, and **institutional racism**. More generally, it is important to acknowledge as well that standards related to such things as normalcy, success, and failure are socially and politically constructed within social and power relationships that are highly unequal and contribute to differential access to valued resources.

An alternative approach that draws from cultural studies, but that also incorporates elements of individual or institutional analysis, consists of **ethnographic studies** and **life histories**. Ethnographic accounts provide a detailed description of the organizational patterns and social activities that constitute the life of a community and its members. Early ethnographic work was dominated by non-Aboriginal anthropologists and other social scientists concerned with documenting the cultural activities of various First Nations, usually based on fieldwork and extended periods of observation or interaction within specific community settings. These relationships sometimes made it possible to present a rich and often sympathetic portrait that drew attention both to everyday life experiences and to complex and diverse forms of social organization that counteracted popular myths about Aboriginal societies (see especially Jenness, 1977). However, other stereotypes were also perpetuated through such work, particularly through portrayals of Aboriginal cultures as primitive museum pieces. Trigger (1985: 47) points to the ways in which these images have been kept alive in school textbooks that draw attention to Native cultures as **prehistoric relics** without any critical analysis of interactions among First Nations, between Aboriginal people and non-Aboriginal newcomers, and in subsequent historical developments: 'The development of native cultures in prehistoric times is treated in an extremely cursory fashion, if at all, and inadequate attention is paid to the dynamism and diverse accomplishments of native people prior to the coming of the first Europeans; and Indians continue to be treated only as part of the setting in which the story of these newcomers unfolds.'

A burgeoning literature, drawn from the experiences and voices of Aboriginal people themselves, counteracts non-Native biases and stereotyping of Aboriginal people. Some of the most striking examples of this work take the form of personal accounts of residential schooling and its impact on people's lives and communities (Assembly of First Nations, 1994; Deiter, 1999; Jaine, 1993; Nuu-chah-nulth Tribal Council, 1996; Treaty 7 Elders and Tribal Council, 1996). Many of these stories are remarkable for how they combine insights into the practices that have contributed to the destabilization of lives, communities, and cultures with a strong sense of agency and resiliency through their struggles to regain and realize their hopes. The Treaty 7 Elders (1996: 159), for example, acknowledge that some members of their nations appreciated that the 'schools taught Indians how to deal with hard times', despite their more common educational experiences:

> The emerging Anglo-Canadian elite was so concerned with its own interests that it was unwilling to make the new institutions and policies work properly to the benefit of the Aboriginal people. Under-funding, incompetent officials, and racial stigma were the issues that the First Nations had to deal with in the post-treaty era.

These accounts, too, reveal how cultures are not abstract phenomena that exist independently of people, but rather are living, **dynamic entities** that interact with and take shape within daily social circumstances. **Culture** in this sense is multi-faceted; it may function as **a tool used by dominant groups** to oppress and undermine the less powerful, or it may be **a resource that people draw upon** to give energy to their lives and identities, or it may be **a vital feature of ongoing social interaction** (Center for Contemporary Cultural Studies, 1982). It must be acknowledged, as well, that even within Aboriginal perspectives, varying degrees of emphasis are given to each of these cultural dimensions. For some, the individual experience is paramount, others assert the need to recapture lost traditions as the cornerstone for Aboriginal autonomy, while still others stress the importance their heritage serves as a basis for forging new relationships between Aboriginal and non-Aboriginal people and agencies.

STRUCTURAL APPROACHES

Representative individual and cultural perspectives have made significant contributions to how we understand Aboriginal people's educational and social experiences. However, these accounts have tended to isolate particular elements of lives and cultures from a thorough analysis of the social, economic, and political contexts in which they occur (Marker, 2000: 30).

Structural approaches to the analysis of Aboriginal education, by contrast, make these contextual elements their central focus. Viewed in this way, the pathways open to people, and the choices made by individuals and agencies, are constrained or even predetermined by their external environments. **Schooling** is oriented to provide individuals with capacities and skills required for **social and economic success**, but it also reflects and reinforces persistent **patterns of inequality**. In these regards, educational practices and outcomes cannot be understood without reference to **policy** frameworks, **labour markets**, and **structures of inequality** that contribute to differential opportunities and outcomes based on social factors like **gender, class**, and **race**. Whether these inequalities and the processes that produce them are deliberate or not, attention must be paid to how social and economic activities are constructed, maintained, or transformed over time.

Theories of **internal colonialism** represent one of the most widely employed structural approaches to the explanation of inequalities between Aboriginal and non-Aboriginal Canadians in education and in other spheres of social life. Akin to institutional analysis, internal colonial models emphasize the mechanisms employed by dominant groups to subordinate or regulate indigenous populations. What distinguishes the internal colonial approach is its characterization of the colonization process as ongoing and deepening rather than temporary or incidental in nature. Cultural differences in themselves are not the primary focus; rather, what matters is how one group or set of interests is able to secure and maintain its advantage over another. Frideres (1998: 3–7) outlines how colonization of indigenous people and lands proceeded in Canada, from initial entry and occupation of the land by Europeans, through destruction and reorganization of Aboriginal societies and cultures, and to regulatory mechanisms, social and economic marginalization, and race-based ideologies.

Several writers identify the education system—through the content and process of schooling as well as the ways in which education systems are organized and governed—as a central force in the continuing colonization of First Nations and other Aboriginal groups. **Aboriginal viewpoints** are frequently absent in **curricula** and the ways in which school programs are structured; educational **policies** and **hiring practices** contribute to an absence or under-representation of Aboriginal people as **teachers, administrators**, and **school board** members; and **government regulations** have constrained the emergence of effective planning, financing, and delivery processes in First Nations initiatives in education and other fields (Angus, 1991: 23–4; Brady, 1992; Common, 1991: 4–5; McPherson, 1991: 11–12; Perley, 1992: 5–6; Perley, 1993).

These observations demonstrate the systemic ways in which governments, policies, and other agencies have contributed to the subordination and destabilization of Aboriginal people and their cultures and communities over time. Fundamental change through which indigenous people are decolonized requires an initial understanding of the embedded nature of colonial processes. Nonetheless, internal colonial models and the assumptions they are grounded in offer an incomplete or inadequate explanation of Aboriginal people's education and social circumstances in several respects. Frideres (1998: 7) suggests that the structural approach is best understood as a model, rather than a theory, enabling us to gain in simplified form a summary of the factors that have produced ongoing inequalities between Aboriginal and non-Aboriginal populations. Once we begin to move beyond this 'shorthand' or vantage point, we must incorporate into our thinking complex interrelationships that cannot fully be encompassed by a colonization framework. In particular, it is necessary to understand the historical dynamics that represent significant modifications or transformations in the nature of colonizing processes over time; strategies of **resistance** and **decolonization** among Aboriginal people; **variations, diversity, and change** within both Aboriginal and non-Aboriginal populations, as well as in the relations among these populations; and **broader social, economic, and policy frameworks** within which these relationships take place (Satzewich and Wotherspoon, 2000: 8–11).

Education has been reassessed more recently from a variety of perspectives in terms of its role and potential for processes of decolonization. Here, the concern is to create conditions to ensure that Aboriginal people have meaningful opportunities to be represented and participate in conventional institutional settings as well as to reconstruct their identities and foster self-determination on their own terms. In some cases, writers have drawn upon Marxism, feminism, or other theoretical alternatives to link indigenous people's struggles with approaches that combine a language of critique that exposes relations of oppression with commitment to fundamental change (see, e.g., Adams, 1990; Slowey, 1999). However, the relationships among these approaches are often uneasy or even hostile, as Marxist or feminist analysis has often been seen to subordinate indigenous vantage points or experiences, or has been unable to account for important forms of diversity within and between populations

(Emberley, 1996; Voyageur, 1996; Wotherspoon, 2003). It is important to acknowledge, as well, that government and educational authorities were not always entirely successful in their efforts to assimilate or subordinate Aboriginal people. Fiske (1996: 181) argues that, while colonial education incorporated practices that were 'harsh, unremittingly sexist, and unilaterally imposed', many Aboriginal people actively resisted these efforts. She illustrates this with reference to Carrier women in central British Columbia, who maintained vibrant family and community relationships by drawing selectively on new skills and forms of leadership that emerged from their schooling experience.

The strongest advocates for decolonization have been Aboriginal scholars and community members, who emphasize that indigenous people can regain control over their lives, identities, and cultures only when they are able to achieve autonomy from Eurocentric thought and institutions. There are various positions within this general stance, reflecting views that range from demands for full sovereignty or self-governance to the creation of distinct 'spaces' within existing organizations. Overall, though, the unifying thread in this analysis is recognition of the deeply embedded nature of colonial hegemony in institutional practices, knowledge, language, and thought. Effective decolonization demands not only that there be Aboriginal personnel and content in schools and other institutions, but that new structures and forms of social interaction are created around indigenous knowledge and world views (Battiste and Henderson, 2000: 92–4).

Colonization processes rely on the **continuous subversion** of indigenous social systems, approaches to knowledge, forms of literacy, and other organized cultural practices, either ignoring them altogether, treating them as primitive and underdeveloped, or undermining them as partial or unrepresentative ways of thinking. Initiatives like the introduction of elements of Aboriginal cultural heritage into the curriculum or the devolution of control over First Nations education from the federal government to bands or tribal councils are important steps towards recognition of the need for greater involvement by Aboriginal people in educational processes and decision-making. However, on their own they may perpetuate colonial processes insofar as they are framed within the language and institutional forms employed by the dominant culture and its agents.

It is difficult, from mainstream vantage points, to appreciate the significance of this last point. Even if many people agree that Aboriginal people should enjoy some rights to special status and self-government, there is a strong sentiment that when Aboriginal people pursue their indigenous heritage and rights too adamantly, and especially if they do not comply with provincial laws and standards in areas like education, they are limiting their options to develop the skills, language, and cultural attributes essential for success in globally competitive societies (Ponting, 1998: 286). The problem with this assessment is that it poses an artificial choice between indigenous heritage and rights and full integration into the mainstream. Certainly, some individuals and organizations within Aboriginal communities advocate this isolationist position, suggesting that indigenous entitlement represents the right to full sovereignty over land, people, and social/cultural systems (McDonnell and Depew, 1999). As we discuss in subsequent chapters, however, most Aboriginal people recognize that their development and contributions can best be fulfilled by having rights, competencies, and opportunities to participate fully in both indigenous and conventional societies. In order to meet this objective, it is essential that Aboriginal people be allocated the 'space' in which they can reconstruct their identities, lives, and communities as part of the process of moving forward into new social relationships and arrangements. Monture-Angus (1999: 26) describes why these steps are necessary, given the deep impact of residential schooling and other colonial legacies:

> To try to address the present-day manifestations of the historical oppression as singular, distinct and individualized, without a clear understanding of colonial causation and the subsequent multiplication of forms of social disorder, is to offer only a superficial opportunity for change and wellness to occur in Aboriginal communities. Such remedies, as they are incomplete, do not offer any real change. The need for historical honesty is not a need to blame others for the present-day realities, but a plea for the opportunity to deal with all of the layers and multiplications of oppression that permeate Aboriginal lives and Aboriginal communities today. When non-Aboriginal guilt becomes the focus of any process meant to address historical wrongs, Aboriginal pain is appropriated and then transformed. This transformation is a recreation of colonial relationships.

Many readers may be tempted to reject concepts like 'oppression' and 'Aboriginal pain' as inappropriate or even offensive, or at least they may not regard them as meaningful, without an understanding of the context in which they are located. This is in part the focus of the next chapter. The point here is not to paint an image of Aboriginal people as defenceless victims, nor to deny that other Canadians have experienced subjugation, humiliation, or deprivation. And, as emphasized earlier, it is important to acknowledge that there are Aboriginal people who occupy, or strive to occupy, relatively privileged positions and circumstances. However, the colonization process overall has forcibly and systematically removed indigenous people from their lands, undermined their family and community support structures, and destroyed individual and community capacity with few opportunities until recently for reconstruction. Monture-Angus (ibid., 51–2) suggests that the reduction of Aboriginal people's concerns to 'social and economic problems' (however significant these are) denies the centrality of legal and social rights to indigenous self-determination at the same time that it trivializes and even reproduces the circumstances in which social conditions became problems or disadvantages. Writing from a non-Aboriginal perspective, Cairns (2000) makes a similar case in his promotion of the concept of 'citizens plus' to acknowledge the development of complementary models of Aboriginal nationhood and Canadian federalism (see also Fleras and Spoonley, 1999, for parallel arguments related to the New Zealand context). It is not possible to develop an adequate understanding of Aboriginal education and future prospects without sensitivity to this broader framework that examines the points where people's lives, identities, options, and choices intersect with social, economic, political, and historical forces.

LINKAGES BETWEEN PERSONAL EXPERIENCES AND SOCIAL STRUCTURES

The analysis that we employ in this book is informed by Aboriginal perspectives as well as by more general views of social participants. In particular, we draw from the voices of survivors of residential schools (in Chapter 3) and children and youth in contemporary provincial and alternative schools (in Chapter 4) in order to examine how schooling has affected the lives, aspirations, and prospects of these Aboriginal people. However, our analysis is linked, as well, to broader contextual analyses of the social, economic, and policy frameworks within which schooling, employment and social prospects, family and community life, and cultural interactions are constituted. Educational practices and outcomes cannot be understood either in isolation from other factors or as mere by-products of the social systems in which they operate. Rather, schooling is one of several crucial, interdependent sites in which people's identities, social interactions, options, and orientations to the world take shape. Although what happens in schools is meaningful quite apart from the external environment, its social contributions make sense only in relation to other dynamic elements within societies, including such features as democratic opportunities for participation, socio-economic inequalities, segmented labour markets, and systemic racial, class, and gender differentiation (Boldt, 1993; Fleras and Elliott, 1996; Frideres, 1998; Marker, 2000; Ponting, 1997; Satzewich and Wotherspoon, 2000).

It is essential to reinforce the observation, as well, that these circumstances are experienced and acted upon in diverse ways within both Aboriginal and non-Aboriginal populations. In other words, while we may be able to make some statistical predictions about a person's life prospects based on social background and characteristics, we must acknowledge that social outcomes and experiences are neither entirely predictable nor fully the product of chance, free will, or other random events. Our analysis is guided, in this, by one of the central insights of the discipline of sociology: that **we make sense of social life through the interactions that take shape between individuals and societies.** Individuals' traits, motivations, and actions have a profound effect on the course that their lives take; however, these factors become meaningful in social contexts produced both through people's direct and indirect interactions with one another and in deeply entrenched patterns of language and meaning, institutions, and underlying social structural arrangements. Our identities, actions, and orientations both shape and are shaped by our social relationships and positions in society.

An analysis that explores **the linkages between individual vantage points and social structures** enables us to move beyond a critique of social arrangements to explore varied prospects for and dimensions of social change. Awareness of **potential for transformations** is vital in thinking about an area such as Aboriginal education, where nearly all commentators, regardless of their theoretical or ideological stances, agree that significant educational improvements are essential for the extension of more general social and economic opportunities throughout the Aboriginal population. That there are several alternative visions of change and strategies to accomplish these changes has been suggested in the preceding brief summary of some major theoretical positions.

Our analysis indicates that effective social transformation cannot be reduced to any single causal factor, whether posed as a matter of individual initiative, increasing cultural sensitivity, or the reorganizing of schools and other institutions. We argue (in Chapter 6) that significant changes can and should be made in schools and in the way they are organized to deliver educational programming and involve Aboriginal people. But the impact of these sorts of changes will be minimal in the absence of more fundamental changes in labour markets and other socio-economic structures that both contribute to and depend on the perpetuation of social inequality.

Schooling itself, as we noted in the Preface, is transformative in nature, for not only does it transmit formal lessons and bestow credentials but it also can be central in developing personalities and identities, in nurturing and advancing our human, social capacities. Schooling is more than simply a set of technical or organizational arrangements. It is also an **interpersonal** and **moral** enterprise, because it involves social relationships and seeks to regulate and modify character or personality. As most observers who have spent any time in a typical school setting—especially, but not exclusively, the early and middle grades—can attest, considerable time and energy are devoted to discipline and behaviour in the classroom and at other school sites. While some of this effort is concerned with establishing social order so that other 'teaching' activities can proceed, school organization is based on assumptions about 'norms'—the nature of normal or desirable **behaviour, personal characteristics**, and **social practices**. These normative frameworks, in turn, are often understood as neutral even though they are deeply ingrained with expectations and practices carried into school through wider social structural elements that tend to be marked by class, gender, race, culture, and other fundamentally **unequal social relations.**

Much of the history of schooling for Aboriginal people in Canada has been marked by distinct efforts to contend with what was, in the view of state and school authorities, a 'problem' of Indian identity and culture. Schooling intervened into people's lives as a mechanism variously (1) to isolate children from their families, and often from other Canadians, or (2) to eradicate the 'Indianness' that was viewed as problematic for official nation-building strategies. Contemporary schooling, oriented more fully to acceptance of Aboriginal people's cultural background and participation in Canadian society, if not to their distinctness as indigenous people, must now grapple with the search for strategies to reconcile this history with the powerful pressures asserted by global economic forces, extensive cultural and social diversity, and political contestation. These themes are explored throughout this book, beginning in the next chapter with an understanding of the legacy left by residential schooling.

CONCLUSION

This chapter has been concerned with theories that help to explain changing education practices for Aboriginal people, with particular emphasis on the persistence of the idea that an 'education gap' exists between Aboriginal people and the general population. A common feature of most theoretical orientations has been their concern to attribute 'blame' for the problem on individuals, conflicting cultural or institutional standards, or the efforts by European colonial authorities, Canadian governments, and other dominant groups to colonize and subordinate indigenous people and their cultures. We have argued that the difficulty in reality is more complex than any of these approaches, in themselves, are able to solve.

The educational pathways that people may follow are highly contingent upon the options and barriers that confront them, and are influenced by a broad array of historical, social, economic, political, cultural, community, and family conditions. Educational opportunities and conditions have been highly constrained for Canadian Aboriginal people by externally imposed policies and practices that have tended to treat indigenous people as objects rather than subjects of their own education, social interests, and futures. It is important, in conceptualizing education and developing educational practices that will allow Aboriginal people to realize their aspirations, to look closely at the impact of both overt and hidden dimensions of schooling processes, and the social forces that give rise to them, and to ensure that Aboriginal voices are an essential part of educational planning and practice.

QUESTIONS FOR CRITICAL THOUGHT

1. In what ways do theories help us to make sense of developments in Aboriginal education?
2. What are the fundamental differences among the main theoretical approaches outlined in this chapter? What are the strengths and limitations of each approach, and what does each offer towards our understanding of the history, contemporary realities, and future prospects for Aboriginal education in Canada?

3. What factors are needed to develop an adequate understanding or explanation of Aboriginal peoples' experiences with education in Canada?
4. Discuss the following statement: 'Effective education change must be grounded in a thorough knowledge of educational practice, but it must also be guided by theory.'
5. Theories help us to explain and predict phenomena, but they also can be
   applied to different political or policy agendas. Discuss the policy implications for Aboriginal education that arise from the main theoretical perspectives outlined in this chapter.

RECOMMENDED READING

Battiste, Marie, ed. 2000. *Reclaiming Indigenous Voice and Vision*. Vancouver:
University of British Columbia Press.

Authors representing a variety of disciplines and national settings outline
the foundations and principles of indigenous knowledge. The book considers the consequences of colonization and provides strategies for decolonization and healing, drawing on education, knowledge, and awareness of the
distinct nature of indigenous thought and its contributions to an understanding of our social and physical worlds.

Cairns, Alan C. 2000. *Citizens Plus: Aboriginal Peoples and the Canadian State*.
Vancouver: University of British Columbia Press.

The author makes a compelling case for a policy framework that locates
Aboriginal rights and self-government within the context of Canadian citizenship. The analysis rejects positions that either deny the special basis of
Aboriginal rights or view these rights as something that transcends the
Canadian Constitution and federal system. Although education is only discussed incidentally, the work is provocative for the challenge it poses to
Aboriginal peoples and other Canadians to join together to create new and
viable institutions that address fundamental social, cultural, and economic
problems.

Livingstone, D.W. 1999. *The Education-Jobs Gap: Underemployment or Economic
Democracy*. Toronto: Garamond Press.

Livingstone offers a strong analysis of the relationship among education,
work, and economic change. Although the book does not make direct reference to Aboriginal people, it details the context within which people develop and have the possibility to use their learning capacities, credentials, and

work options. Contrary to conventional perspectives on the linkages between education and jobs, the author's analysis reveals that people possess considerable and increasing knowledge and credentials that do not fully factor into the employment options available to them.

Monture-Angus, Patricia. 1995. *Thunder in My Soul: A Mohawk Woman Speaks.* Halifax: Fernwood.

The author integrates her personal experiences in education, law, and politics with a powerful analysis of the conditions and prospects facing Aboriginal people more broadly. The book demonstrates the many faces and legacies of colonization, but points to the possibility of moving forward to new understandings and relationships.

Satzewich, Vic, and Terry Wotherspoon. 2000. *First Nations: Race, Class, and Gender Relations.* Regina: Canadian Plains Research Centre.

This is one of the few works that develops a distinct theoretical framework for the analysis of Aboriginal people and their relations with the Canadian state and social institutions. It employs a critical political economy perspective to show how changing economic and policy structures, in conjunction with gender, class, and race relations, have affected the circumstances and life chances of Aboriginal people. It highlights the contradictory nature of education, as well as of other institutional realms such as work, health care, and the welfare and criminal justice systems, and examines the organized struggles by Aboriginal people to engage in critical decision-making.

❖

CHAPTER 3

THE LEGACY OF
RESIDENTIAL SCHOOLS

INTRODUCTION

Our intention in this chapter is to describe the history of Aboriginal education in Canada in residential schools in order to explain better education's historical role in the subjugation of Aboriginal people. Our
approach is twofold: to describe history through the eyes of the survivors
in both primary and secondary accounts; and to place this history in an
explanatory context that includes issues of state hegemony over First
Nations people and the Euro-Canadian quest to industrialize Canada.

Most clearly, our arguments are based on the contention that the history of the relations between Aboriginal peoples and formal education in
Canada is largely a history of cultural genocide. This fact is becoming
increasingly clear as First Nations survivors of residential schools are
making their voices heard in two ways. First, continuing lawsuits against
the federal government and churches of Canada are based on a quest by
residential school survivors for compensation for sexual and physical
abuse in residential schools. Second, a growing body of relatively new
research is documenting not only the abuses against Aboriginal children
and youth but also the connections among those abuses, the historical
official policy of assimilation, and the current dilemmas faced by
Aboriginal peoples and communities.

The journey that we embark upon here is one framed by Santayana's
aphorism that if we do not study and reflect upon history, then we will be
condemned to repeat it. The history of such genocide might best be
described in terms of cultural destruction, although there are writers of
Aboriginal ancestry who believe that the history of residential schools is
a history of absolute genocide. What we study here is the worst and most
blatant form of schooling—as a tool of control, exploitation, and destruction. The residential school system attempted to assimilate Canadian First
Nations children into a Euro-Canadian culture and economic system,

ironically through the practice of isolating them for gradual integration at a later phase of development. In this quest, what it meant to be of First Nations ancestry was obliterated and replaced with a rigid code of temporal, linguistic, and religious/moral conduct that fed the political and economic needs of an expanding, colonizing economic Goliath. We demonstrate through this historical account that until recently the role of education in the lives of Aboriginal peoples in Canada has not changed significantly since the early twentieth century. What changes have occurred are of form and degree; the impact of those changes has remained largely unchanged. School, for the most part, has been a place where Aboriginal children have done less well than their non-Aboriginal counterparts and where public explanations for this fact have been reduced to issues of race, class, and culture. Later, we consider how the media played a role in constructing social problems faced by Aboriginal peoples as problems resulting from lack of educational success.

We draw for the information in this chapter on some very poignant and valuable sources, including Jim Miller's *Shingwauk's Vision: A History of Residential Schools in Canada*, Roland Chrisjohn's *The Circle Game*, Isabelle Knockwood's *Out of the Depths*, and the graduate thesis of Helen Cote, 'Damaged Children and Broken Spirits: An Examination of Attitudes of Anisnabe Elders to Acts of Violence Among Anisnabe Youth in Saskatchewan'. The latter two works, both of which are first-person accounts of victimization and exploitation as opposed to official accounts based on a polemic of educational rights, connect the damage wrought by the education of Indian children with the modern-day dilemmas faced by Aboriginal peoples. The historical and autobiographical accounts that we draw on focus attention on a theoretical perspective that goes beyond understanding the exploitation of Aboriginal children and youth in residential school as a result of internal colonialism (Frideres, 1998; Miller, 1996) or cultural genocide (Chrisjohn and Young, 1997). This historical perspective, then, is based on a theory of absolute genocide in which the destruction of culture and the enslavement or protracted physical destruction of a people are a planned state project. Canada's First Nations peoples were in the way of the relentless onrush of capitalist and industrial expansion (York, 1992). By the late nineteenth century, their protracted destruction was undertaken most forcefully with compulsory Euro-Canadian education. The legacy is one of continuing harm, albeit in a more subtle guise. This chapter is an attempt to understand how modern universal education is a logical political-economic extension of the residential school era in the 'development' of Canada.

We acknowledge, however, that a somewhat dated body of 'neo-colonialist' literature, written mostly by non-Aboriginal social commentators, stands in contradiction to the history we present here. This literature is based on several partial or incomplete sources: individual histories of missionaries among the 'Indians' (e.g., Nock, 1988, *A Victorian Missionary and Canadian Indian Policy*); American history applied to the Canadian context (e.g., Coleman's 1993 *American Indian Children at School, 1850–1930*); and literature reviews of selected scholarly works that 'prove' that despite what has happened to Aboriginal people in the past, they have become like white people and that is the only reality we need to face (e.g., Richards, 2000, 'Reserves Are Only Good for Some People'). These works represent for us an ongoing scholarly and social discourse that is a fundamental part of the injustice Aboriginal people suffer. Nock's work tells us that there were good missionaries; Coleman tells us, in a traditional anthropological paradigm, that Aboriginal students in boarding schools in America were ambivalent about their experiences; and Richards describes how even the most progressive scholars perceive modern-day Aboriginal culture as rightly assimilated into the socio-economic system through which we all gain advantage. Certainly there are truths in these works. It would be naive to assume that all missionaries were bad, that all children in residential school suffered severely, or that assimilation is not part of the reality for race relations in Canada.

In practice, as with most forms of formal education, residential schooling and its outcomes and consequences have had mixed and often contradictory significance. Many government and educational officials, even if they had low estimations of the capacities of Aboriginal children, were committed to offering training, skills, and discipline that would be useful for integration into selected strata within Canadian society. In most cases, students were expected to combine studies with practical training oriented to domestic work, farm labour, or other trades. This meant that students' academic progress was limited, often complicated further by the absence of meaningful employment opportunities out of school. In a few instances church officials sponsored students to continue their studies at the post-secondary level, but state authorities were more likely to place severe restrictions on registered Indian students' abilities to advance their education and frequently refused students' requests for more formal education (Barman et al, 1986: 9–13; Stevenson, 1991: 222–3). Residential schools, despite their damaging consequences for community relations, sometimes constituted a basis for friendships, personal connections, resistance, and political organization (Fiske, 1996). Accounts of residential schooling are further mixed by acknowledgement that schooling (though not necessarily in the form that it took in residential schools) was sought, or at least regarded as a necessary evil, by many Aboriginal people as a vehicle through which their children and communities would gain a chance to survive in a modernizing world (see, e.g., Treaty 7 Elders and Tribal Council, 1996: 155–61). Moreover, not all Aboriginal children experienced residential schooling—not all children, and especially Aboriginal children, attended any kind of school regularly in the late nineteenth and early twentieth centuries; residential schools were not a factor in many communities, which often had day schools; and the federal government was not responsible for the education of non-status and Métis children.

Nonetheless, the overall impact of residential schooling, hidden until recently in denial, isolation, or sublimated memories, has been highly destructive for individuals, their families, and Aboriginal communities in general. By focusing on a few successes or good stories, the social commentators/historians who cast a positive light on residential schooling either miss or fail to acknowledge the socio-economic forces that continue to put Aboriginal people in their 'place'.

We emphasize, in addition and without apology, that if we continue to ignore the voices of those most damaged, we are part of the problem and not part of the solution. The strong works we include in this chapter are written largely, although not entirely, by Aboriginal people and, most importantly, by Aboriginal scholars/writers who have tried to make sense of their first-hand experiences of oppression. Some of the works that we do not discuss in this chapter, such as Celia Haig-Brown's (1988) *Resistance and Renewal: Surviving the Residential School* and Linda Jaine's (1993) *Residential School: The Stolen Years*, incorporated some of the initial autobiographical accounts by Aboriginal writers and stand as further testimony to how important the first-hand Aboriginal experience is in taking a radical new view of Canadian history. We would be remiss as non-Aboriginal writers if we did not defer to the wisdom and knowledge of Aboriginal writers as the most valid chroniclers of their own oppression. We also wish to state that the conventional literature that we mention above stands in stark contrast to some very fine legal writers who, as knowledgeable observers of the law, present a history of Aboriginal-European relations in Canada that is consonant with the writings of

Aboriginal people. We refer specifically to Thomas Berger (1991), a lawyer and judge who has been involved in Royal Commissions on northern development and who has written an important legal-historical work on Native rights in the Americas: *A Long and Terrible Shadow: White Values, Native Rights in the Americas, 1492–1992*; Patricia Monture-Angus (1995), a Mohawk legal scholar and activist who documents the colonialist nature of the Canadian legal system in *Fire in My Soul: A Mohawk Woman Speaks*; Rupert Ross (1992, 1996), who practises law in northern Manitoba and who describes the human rights damages incurred by Aboriginal people as they come into contact with formal law in *Dancing with a Ghost* and *Returning to the Teachings*; and Judges A.C. Hamilton and C.M. Sinclair (1991), who led the Manitoba Aboriginal Justice Inquiry.

INDOCTRINATION AND DESTRUCTION OF SELF, COMMUNITY, AND FAMILY

To understand how education, both historically and in contemporary circumstances, has helped to maintain state control over Aboriginal peoples, we need to discover what was lost to First Nations communities through compulsory education. It is important to realize that all cultures and civilizations have some form of education, and that pre-contact First Nations peoples had forms of education though they might be unfamiliar to many Canadians. Their education was based on experiential, informal learning that was integrated with life and was not based on notions of competition for marks or grades or on attaining specified levels of achievement. Education was preparation for life. This stands in contrast to public or formal education systems today that originated in the nineteenth- and twentieth-century residential schools and the manual labour schools developed by Egerton Ryerson and other prominent school promoters. The implicit assumption in this institutional education paradigm is that education prepares the developing child for the labour market. Interestingly, Aboriginal peoples' current struggles to reclaim their culture and dignity often involve reclaiming traditional forms of learning.

> The dignity of Aboriginal culture was lost initially through forms of discipline in residential schools that attacked the implicit sense of autonomy in Aboriginal cultures.
> The ethic of non-interference is the essence of Aboriginal cultures,

and is probably one of the oldest and one of the most pervasive of all the ethics by which we Indians live. It has been practiced for twenty-five or thirty thousand years, but it is not very well-articulated. . . . This principle essentially means that an Indian will never interfere in any way with the rights, privileges and activities of another person. . . . Interference in any form is forbidden, regardless of the following irresponsibilities or mistakes that your brother is going to make. (Ross, 1992: 12)

This fundamental principle of life was extended to children and stood in direct contrast to the use of coercion, physical or emotional discipline, ridicule, or any other form of behaviour modification that came to be the trademark of both residential schools and, in a more muted form, modern-day conventional education.

That Aboriginal cultures cherished individual autonomy and expression was manifested in an ethos of learning described as the three 'L's—looking, listening, and learning (Miller, 1996). This method of acquiring knowledge relied on the use of models and illustrations through storytelling and rested on a belief system that the eldest in the community had the wisdom to offer and that they were to be listened to with respect. As such, the process of learning was devoid of coercion and routine and respected the giver and the receiver. The acquisition of vocational and life skills was based on observation and emulation and was carried out in a context without institutional structure and that blended education and play. This system stands in stark contrast to modern-day conventional education that is highly routine, tends to divorce education from fun, and is eminently institutionalized.

For children from societies in which education occurred in informal and informally structured ways, the schooling regime that the abortive missionary efforts of New France attempted to impose on them was simply unbearable. The alien quality of regimented hours, indoor classrooms, structured lessons, and a competitive ethos were for most of these children foreign, stressful, and painful in the highest degree (ibid., 57).

The imposition of a compulsory system of formalized education created not only generations of traumatized children and youth, but also young people who were unable to survive in either world. They were inculcated with Euro-Canadian values and regimens that, they were told, had to become part of the way they lived. This newly acquired code of conduct left many students marginal from both cultures; they were unable to fit into their culture of origin and were always outsiders in the dominant Euro-Canadian society. When those sorts of emotional confusion are added to the loss of the traditional lands and territories, the individuals' sense of self is under extreme stress. York (1992), in *The Dispossessed*, describes how rapid industrialization and the expropriation of Aboriginal lands and communities in Canada in the 1850s and 1860s eroded Aboriginal communities to the point of extinction.

In a section on children and gas-sniffing York (ibid., 17) makes connections between industrial exploitation and education in the context of Aboriginal Australians:

> For centuries, the Children of Elcho Island were educated by their relatives. Today the Western educational system has intruded, cutting across the responsibilities of the aboriginal adults and placing a barrier between man and boy . . . the aboriginal adolescent is doubly excluded. On the one hand he is blocked from sharing in the benefits of European society by educational deficiencies and by the fear of breaking step; on the other, he is ambivalent about many of the old ways. Some he has forgotten altogether. . . . Gasoline sniffing is a result of the disorientation of the Murngin adolescents. . . . Adolescents reflect the conflicts of a people.

In this simple, poignant example, we see how cultural invasion through education had a direct and profound effect on the welfare of children and youth. The problem of gas-sniffing is ubiquitous among exploited communities in North America and Australia and the question is still being asked why gasoline-sniffing has taken over the lives of young people in communities like Elcho Island in Australia or Davis Inlet, Labrador.

On 26 January 1993, six Inuit youth in Davis Inlet tried to commit suicide together by sniffing gasoline. Their attempt at collective suicide was thwarted by an addictions counselor who heard the youth declare that they wanted to die. Subsequently, 14 youth from this small community were airlifted south for medical treatment, but the legacy of colonization and government neglect remained. Ninety-five per cent of the adult population were addicted to alcohol, 10 per cent of the children and youth were chronic gasoline-sniffers, and 25 per cent of the adults had attempted suicide. Nearly a decade later, the trauma for Davis Inlet has grown. In November 2000, 20 Innu children were airlifted to the Goose Bay treatment centre as an interim reaction to another epidemic of gas-sniffing among the children. Of the 169 children aged 10–19 living in Davis Inlet at the end of 2000, 154 have attempted gas-sniffing and 70 of them are chronic sniffers. The socio-economic reality for Davis Inlet, like that for many other northern Aboriginal communities in Canada (York, 1992), is one of historical resource exploitation and/or community relocation, and the imposition of 'industrial education'.

Helen Cote, an Anisnabe elder and scholar from Saskatchewan, presents another dimension of the problem as she explains how her family became unrecognizable to her after she and her siblings were forcibly removed to residential school. Her father, who had never had a drink in his life, began to drink after his children were taken, and his alcohol abuse resulted in the destruction of his marriage. In returning to her family of origin after years of absence, she was not only a different person to her family but her family was no longer there, at least as a loving, nurturing unit. The historical works and personal stories of the connection between education and family illustrate a fundamental reality of forcibly imposed, compulsory education. Inappropriate education not only destroys children and youth, it also destroys families and communities. Whether such communities were doomed to destruction because of unbridled resource exploitation from the 1940s onward is a subject that might also be debated. But, it is clear that a Euro-Canadian-based compulsory education model imposed on Aboriginal peoples certainly contributed to a type of cultural genocide that some commentators argue still exists.

INDENTURED LABOUR

The question remains, then, that if the government of Canada and various churches and agencies undoubtedly saw this destruction taking place, how could they persist with a system that they knew full well would destroy culture so completely? The answer lies in some critical work that has linked the role of residential schools and government policy bent on the forced assimilation of Aboriginal people to the facilitation of a growing industrial-based labour market. The most critical of these works (York, 1992; Satzewich and Wotherspoon, 2000) make the argument that policies towards Aboriginal people, including education policy, were a calculated, albeit veiled, expropriation of Aboriginal rights and indenture of Aboriginal peoples, linked with the expansion of industry and resource markets. Even the Royal Commission on Aboriginal Peoples (1996b: 335) was clear in its assessment of imposed education:

Put simply, the residential school system was an attempt by successive governments to determine the fate of Aboriginal people in Canada by appropriating and reshaping their future in the form of thousands of children who were removed from their homes and communities and placed in the care of strangers. Those strangers, the teachers and staff, were, according to Hayter Reed, a senior member of the department in the 1890s, to employ 'every effort . . . against anything calculated to keep fresh in the memories of the children habits and associations which it is one of the main objects of industrial education to obliterate.' Marching out from the schools, the children, effectively re-socialized, imbued with the values of European culture, would be the vanguard of a magnificent metamorphosis: the 'savage' was to be made 'civilized,' made fit to take up the privileges and responsibilities of citizenship.

In essence, the expressed intent of residential school policy was to destroy a culture and rebuild Indian children as active participants in the industrial economy, if not remove them as impediments to economic development. The unapologetic attempt to destroy culture was an extreme expression of an assimilationist mentality that persists to the present. The patriarchal nature of education as part of this assimilationist movement began essentially with the development of manual labour schools proposed by Egerton Ryerson. Ryerson and other representatives of parochial institutions developed industrial labour schools for Aboriginal children based on principles of basic education, hard work, and religious devotion, values that were held sacred by the Euro-Canadian middle class. The order of the manual labour school was the principle of 'half-day' in which the student would be exposed to academics in the morning and would spend the rest of the day acquiring the practical labour skills—farming and mechanics for boys and domestic skills for girls—that would allow them to exist in an industrialized world. Clearly, one of the expressed purposes of the half-day system was to allow students to contribute to the maintenance and expansion of the school. Ultimately, Ryerson and other government officials envisioned the residential labour schools as potentially self-sufficient. As the self-sufficiency of these schools did not come to fruition, the expense of maintaining them was downloaded by the government to the Christian churches.

It is at this point in the history of Aboriginal education in Canada that historians tend to disagree. The conventional historical accounts generally focus on the assimilationist demands of the federal government as part of a program whereby the schools would function as instruments of economic and cultural absorption. Moreover, the mandate of the missionary movements in Canada was to induce conformity not only to religious beliefs but, more importantly, to the daily rituals of obedience and subservience. Indeed, the same values and expectations applied to white society, especially the working classes. Government officials saw parochial residential schools, then, as 'social laboratories in which a people's beliefs and ways could be refashioned' (Miller, 1996: 119). This reading, although not entirely inaccurate, presumes that an assimilationist mentality pervaded the ways of thinking of government and religious bureaucrats.

While this may have been true, in part, a more careful and complete reading of this history focuses on the physical and sexual exploitation that occurred almost regularly in most residential schools. For example, the forced schooling of registered Indian children at the end of the nineteenth century was based on a system of apprenticeship that provided free child and youth labour for farms, industries, and households (Miller, 1996). As we shall see, this sort of servitude was common among all marginalized groups, including impoverished immigrant white children. This involuntary servitude extended well into the middle of the twentieth century with the system of outing in which Aboriginal children in residential schools were sent to work on farms and in domestic situations as seasonal free labour. Miller (1996) documents how, in many cases, all able-bodied students were pulled out of school to help with the local harvest or to engage in the cutting of wood prior to winter. Similarly, girls were extracted from school to work in local homes under the guise of work experience. However, school and government officials believed that domestic labour would not only provide badly needed labour for the community but that it would keep girls 'out of trouble' from the sexual advances of peers and from potentially compromising innocent schoolteachers. This racist and ageist belief system condemned not only Aboriginal children and youth as sexually volatile but also placed the blame for sexual indiscretion squarely on the shoulders of the children and youth as potential predators and teachers as potential victims. The attendant presumption was that girls and boys, because of their sexual volatility, could not be trusted to be together. While this was true in non-Aboriginal schools also, the mistrust of children's sexuality was particularly acute in residential schools. Physical distancing was the practice based on a long-standing mistrust of children and youth as incompletely socialized beings. Interestingly, the distancing of girls and boys in education persists somewhat today in school settings where physical education and sex education classes are segregated, where sports teams are stratified by gender, and where technical and academic subjects are typified by high enrolments of one or the other gender.

The system of free child and youth labour was important to the vitality of local communities to the extent that communities aggressively lobbied to have schools established in their areas (Miller, 1996). The city of Brandon, in 1891, for example, offered a free site to secure a Methodist residential school. Civic officials saw the industrial or boarding school as a mechanism to 'generate employment, a demand for goods, and a revenue for their community' (ibid., 117). As importantly, the desire for free child and youth labour among these aggressive and growing communities was left unspoken but was nonetheless part of the compulsion to attract residential schools. Furthermore, as Ottawa realized that Indian boarding schools were becoming a burden to the taxpayer, a per capita funding formula was introduced that would decrease spending and enhance revenues. The only way this could happen, in reality, however, was for principals of the schools to reduce spending on food and to increase the labour of the students. As a result, the schools became increasingly unattractive to Aboriginal parents: 'More labour was expected of students, while simultaneously the school sought to limit the food they were receiving. . . . Many Indian groups were more reluctant than ever to surrender their children to the school' (ibid., 128). As a result, missionaries pressured Ottawa to introduce compulsory attendance in Indian schools. This became a reality in 1894 and 1895 with amendments to the Indian Act that gave Indian agents the authority of the law to force Indian children under 16 to go to school.

The conditions of children in residential schools deteriorated dramatically after the turn of the century as compulsory attendance and fiscal priority created schools that were inadequate physical facilities and unprepared and incapable of caring for the health problems of children. Denominational rivalry and competition for students as commodities were responsible for the plague of ill health that beset Indian children. As government official R.H. McKay grudgingly admitted, 'The existence of the school is made to depend on the Government Grant, and if healthy children cannot be secured then the unhealthy are taken in to the destruction of all' (cited ibid., 132).

This system of child and youth slavery under the guise of mandatory education had historical parallels with other social histories of children in

Canada. At the same time, and extending well into the twentieth century, the treatment of immigrant Irish children in Canada was no less savage. Well into the twentieth century, youth who were apprehended by legal authorities were largely white male youth who had little schooling, were poorly nurtured, and who lived primarily on the streets. These 'street urchins' or 'street arabs', as they were called at the time, came from impoverished urban families who were either of first- or second-generation immigrant backgrounds. Further, between 1873 and 1903, over 95,000 children came to Canada from the slums and orphanages of Great Britain (Carrigan, 1998). The policy of importing disadvantaged children reflected a mutual agreement between the governments of Canada and Britain to help 'solve' the wayward children problem in Britain while providing 'indentured servants for Canada's bourgeoisie and as free labour for Canada's expanding industrial sector involving agricultural settlement, the fur trade, and westward expansion' (Schissel, 1993: 8). The reality for most of these children, however, was that they lived at the mercy of their adoptive families in Canada, and the historical records suggest that they were, in general, highly exploited (see, e.g., Kramer and Mitchell, 2002).

The rise of public panic over a growing youth problem in Canada at the turn of the century coincided with the exploitation of children and youth as a form of slave labour. Thus, the movements to free children and youth from the shackles of exploitation took two contradictory forms. The child-saving movement was at the same time bent on preventing the exploitation of children and youth on the streets and in industry, and a movement that, through legislation such as the Juvenile Delinquents Act (1908), tended to label the working and marginal classes as inferior and potentially criminal (Schissel, 1993). Children 'at risk' were identified by their social characteristics and were to be 'saved' by their bourgeois benefactors. The moral panic—that a growing subpopulation of children and youth was becoming increasingly criminogenic and posed an immediate threat to individual and collective welfare—became legitimated by public policy. West (1984: 27) observes that:

> Whereas, during early industrialization, children were grossly exploited for low wages, their partial humanitarian exclusion from the labour market had by the end of the nineteenth century made them an expendable surplus population, a nuisance about which something had to be done. Burgeoning slum areas, the enforced idleness resulting from

the passage of the anti-child labour legislation, 'foreign' immigration, and fears of impending social disorder through epidemics and street crime focused attention on the working-class young (although there were other problems, such as alcoholism, poverty, urban boredom . . .).

In the middle of nineteenth century, Egerton Ryerson and other social reformers who were influential in the development of residential schools for Aboriginal peoples were also of the opinion that Canada was vulnerable to evils of immigrant children and youth. His expressed opinion was that immigrants from the Irish famine 'accompanied by disease and death' were likely the 'harbingers of a worse pestilence of social insubordination and disorder' (Prentice, 1977: 56). As with residential schools for Aboriginal children, social reformers such as Ryerson envisioned universal compulsory education as the panacea for crime, delinquency, and other forms of social unrest at the hands of the marginalized. The justification for forced compliance was easy—the children and youth who fell prey to the law and ended up in youth and adult institutions were identifiable by their socio-economic and racial backgrounds. The tenor of the times dictated that problems of crime and deviance were easily explained by the incompleteness of those who were different. Beginning with John A. Macdonald's move to establish off-reserve residential schools in 1879, a similar belief system framed the movement to force Indian children into a European educational system. Macdonald's appointee, Nicholas Flood Davin, set out to establish a policy of 'aggressive civilization' for Aboriginal peoples based on an expressed belief that 'western Indians were merely at an earlier stage of evolution than their white brothers and sisters' (Miller, 1996: 102).

This is where we see the historical role of education as purposeful of more than assimilation. In fact, education was part of the post hoc justification for enslavement of children and youth in an expanding industrial Canada. Immigrant children were a source of free domestic and agrarian labour. Aboriginal children in residential schools were similarly a source of free labour for the expansion of Christianity and for the subordination of First Nations people who were 'in the way' of Canadian industrialization. Whether educators were deliberately or inadvertently compliant with industry in the exploitation of the labour of children and youth, what started as the use of an untapped labour supply turned into a protracted attack on Aboriginal communities (York, 1992) and an ongoing denigration of the poor and marginalized through associated institutions like the law. It is no coincidence that in the early twentieth century publicly financed correctional facilities for juvenile delinquents were developed to assist schools in controlling young offenders who were on the streets and were neglected (West, 1984). It is also no accident that residential schools were based on the utopian models of prisons that advocated hard labour, discipline, religion, and solitary meditation. The original Cherry Hill and Auburn prisons in the United States and Kingston Penitentiary in Canada were based on penal philosophies that advocated strict discipline, hard labour, and meagre living conditions. In the end, the residential schools were run like modern-day youth and adult prisons in Canada in which time is rigidly controlled, segregation is used as punishment and 'rehabilitation', and the authority structures are unyielding (Morin, 2001).

In Saskatchewan, the majority of prisoners are of Aboriginal ancestry and there is some evidence that modern-day prisons house the irreparably damaged products of residential schools. Although residential schools have been closed for several decades, Cote (2001), a survivor of residential school who has interviewed other survivors, shows how victimization in childhood impairs the ability to be effective and happy parents. As she argues, she and her peers were so damaged by the experiences of forced education that they became chronically involved in the criminal justice system to their own detriment but also to the detriment of their children and grandchildren. Her arguments, then, are based on an understanding of the history of forced education as part of the 'history of genocide'. Whether such a historical reading is accurate or not is debatable, but what cannot be questioned is the veracity of victims of residential schools, who understand their personal histories as encompassing an attack on themselves and a fatal assault on their culture.

EDUCATIONAL IDEOLOGY AND THE LEGITIMATION OF COERCION

The discourse of education is fraught with elaborate rationalizations that perpetuate the philosophy that no one can survive in the modern world without basic conventional education. The extension of this axiom is that the moral obligation of any modern state is to provide its citizens with equal opportunity through established, customary education. The moral view of education as mandatory contains an interesting contradiction, as we shall see as we explore the historical legitimation for residential schools. The arguments are that moral obligation drives the teacher/ administrator and moral learning is the result for the student.

The belief that morality and education are inextricably intertwined provided the basis for the involvement of churches in the operation of residential schools. The federal government, in 1879, commissioned a study headed by Nicholas Flood Davin (cited in Miller, 1996: 102) to provide a template for establishing residential schools in western Canada. The ensuing report provides a not-so-outdated logic for the forced education of Indian children:

> these new establishments should be denominational for two reasons. First, it would be irresponsible to deprive Indians of 'their simple Indian mythology' by a process of 'civilization,' without putting something positive and uplifting in its place. Second, reliance on churches would make it less difficult to find teachers with the essential combination of learning and virtue, and, moreover, to secure their services at a rate of remuneration less than the teachers' qualifications, pedagogical and moral, would otherwise command . . . to teach semi-civilized children is a more difficult task than to teach children with inherited aptitudes, whose training, moreover is carried on at home . . . . The advantage of calling in the aid of religion is that there is a chance of getting an enthusiastic person, with, therefore, a motive power beyond any pecuniary remuneration could supply.

The discourses of learning and virtue, of family involvement, and of the dedicated teacher with missionary zeal are part of the logic of compulsory education that frames education policy today. The presumptions are:

1. that teaching is a moral crusade and that the best teachers are on a moral mission of which money is not a part;
2. that aptitude is inherited and that aptitudes are more prominent among certain sectors of the society;
3. that the best families help in the schooling of children at home;
4. that compulsory education has a spiritual/moral element that is required by all children, but especially those children most unlike the norm.

All of these elements, in some form or another, frame modern-day education exemplified by family values rhetoric in political debates, by a collective common-sense perception that teachers are under-worked and overpaid, and by the continued lobby to keep or reintroduce Christian prayer in schools (despite the fact that such a practice violates the Charter of Rights and Freedoms).

The ideology of education lived, as well, in the labour-school mentality of residential advocates and practitioners. The survivors of residential school we consulted are unanimous in their belief that the schools were primarily about exploiting labour. Isabelle Knockwood describes her and other Mi'kmaw children's experiences in residential school in Nova Scotia. She is very clear that schools deliberately did little to educate Mi'kmaw children because they needed the children and youth to carry out manual labour. She describes how the farm and the physical plant of the school were maintained by the exploited labour of students at the expense of their education:

> The older boys who tended the furnace never went to classes except of course Sunday school. The other boys who were not working in the barn were taken out of school during the coal-shoveling season for weeks at a time until all the coal was put in the bins. Then they returned to classes only to be called out again to work in the fields spreading manure, picking rocks, harvesting vegetables, or slaughtering animals. Their classroom hours were very irregular and an afternoon session once or twice a week was the average. Full-time barn and furnace boys worked fifteen hours a day, seven days a week. (Knockwood, 1992: 58)

She also describes vividly how many of the girls in residential school suffered the same types of work exploitation as domestic help and how an inordinate number of girls and boys were hurt on the job, some severely. A parallel epidemic of injuries of children and youth in employment has been documented in more recent times for agricultural labour and for the fast-food industry (Schissel, 2001; Parker, 1997; Dunn and Runyan, 1993).

The question remains how a so-called civilized society, especially one that had been assumed to be highly moral and virtuous, could treat children as if they were unworthy of human rights. This is the point at which the rhetoric of labour, education, and racism comes to the fore. Compulsory schooling was a highly effective ideological system of self-justification and it drew upon racist and religious/moral beliefs to indict First Nations families and their children and ultimately to confine them to a white world. Indian children were not only considered intellectually inferior to their Euro-Canadian counterparts, but their morality was constantly diminished as a justification for educational control. Schools were seen as social laboratories in which education and hard labour were considered panacea for cultural inferiority. Residential school administrators as well as government officials often held the belief that the Indian child had the capacity to be a responsible citizen but lacked the morality that education would induce. As Miller (1996: 154) contends, 'it seemed clear to many missionaries that the innately intelligent Native children lacked only instruction and enhancement of their underdeveloped moral senses. . . . Native morality was sufficiently debased to justify missions in general and residential schools for their children in particular.'

One of the great ironies of forced education and one of its tragic legacies is that ambiguous attitudes about the capabilities of Aboriginal children resulted in schools that were largely dysfunctional pedagogically. This was the result of institutionalized bigotry that had, at its core, a system of education based on curricula that were ineffective and intentionally dismissive, a system that was staffed by teachers who were poorly trained, incompetent, and in some respects morally bankrupt, and a system based on severe degrees of reward and punishment that violated the human dignity of the schools' charges. Knockwood (1992: 81) describes the reality of punishment for Aboriginal children in residential school:

I remember those horrifying years as if it were yesterday. There was one nun, Sister Gilberta, she always passed out the punishment. Every day, she would take me into the bathroom and lock the door. She would then proceed to beat me thirty times on each hand, three times a day, with a strap. She would count to thirty, out loud, each time she hit me. It's an awful way to learn to count to 30. My older sister, Grace, learned to count to 50.

I never understood why I had to get those beatings, but at the age of 37, I realize it had to be because I spoke my language. To this day, I can't speak my language very well. But I do understand when I am spoken to in Micmac.

Why was our language and culture such a threat that it had to be take away from us with such vengeance?

To be taught your language with respect and kindness by your people, then to have the White Man pull it from your heart with meanness and torture. Some people wonder why we are so tough, because we had to, we had no choice.

I have polio and it affected my bladder and as a child, I wet my pants a lot. I received extra beatings for that too.

Once I was thrown across the dorm floor by Sister Gilberta. At the age of six, it seemed far away. I bounced off the wall at the other end of the dorm. I was sore on one side of my body for a few days.

Cote (2001) further illustrates how punishment was often sexualized to provide the most devastating form of opprobrium:

As we approached the school I became more excited, talking as loudly as I could. The priest turned me over to a nun, who took me upstairs to the infirmary and took my clothes off. She went to fill a bath tub with water. She was very rough, told me to shut up and called me a dirty, filthy, little Indian. My family had never told me to shut up. When I was first told to shut up, it shocked me. Where did she get all these terrible words from? She was pulling my hair, and kept telling me to shut up and to stand still. I fought back. Nobody was going to treat me like dirt. When I protested that she was hurting my head by pulling my long hair, she became more angry and pulled my hair harder. I jumped up to leave, but she knocked me down in the tub. I could never have guessed in a million years what she would do next. She began to scrub me up and down my body, separated my legs and began poking her fingers in my vagina. I was shocked and I protested more by jumping out of the tub and yelling. She slapped me in the face and pulled my hair harder, calling me a dirty little savage. 'We have to clean you inside and out.' She held me down under water several times while she continued to beat me. She almost drowned me. I am sure she would have if I had continued to resist her. Even today, I have nightmares about escaping from water. Such fear of water has been so terrifying for me that I have never learned how to swim.

These graphic accounts of horror are part of a massive body of evidence that residential schools were not places of socialization and learning but rather places where abject behaviourism and sexual exploitation became the institutional mode of operation (Cote, 2001; Jaine, 1993; Miller, 1996; Milloy, 1999; Haig-Brown, 1988; Knockwood, 1992). Education and care were secondary to order, discipline, and sexual exploitation, and this was further evidenced by staff that were poorly qualified and who received little scrutiny upon hiring. As Miller (1996) observes, the use of incompetent or poorly trained teachers was noted as early as 1890 and continued until the 1960s. Residential schools were considered a last resort for most teachers, and the ones that were drawn to Aboriginal schools because of missionary zeal often felt that 'the proper missionary spirit was more important in a potential teacher than normal school or university training in teaching methods' (Miller, 1996: 174). Governments, in their determination to download the financial burden of residential school education to the churches, were all too willing to participate in this implicit policy of inferior education for Aboriginal students. Both governments and churches realized that qualified teachers were expensive and that the pittance the federal government provided for residential schools necessarily dictated that qualified teachers were unaffordable.

The lack of qualified staff and institutionalized racism conspired to create a further dilemma for the lives and futures of the students. Schools unwittingly or knowingly created curricula that focused on the institutional needs and deficient requirements of unqualified teachers. Therefore, no attempt was made to incorporate issues sensitive to the socio-cultural background of the students. Specifically, course content focused on Euro-Canadian history and settlement; the Indian in Canada, in this 'white' history, was always posed as the enemy. Despite the fact that many educational officials were aware of the need to incorporate Aboriginal culture and sensitivity into curricula, the pedagogical materials were decidedly Euro-Canadian, with little recognition of the role of First Nations people in Canadian history as other than 'the enemy'. As Milloy (1999: 175) argues, 'The literary curriculum was education's own worst enemy. The textbooks that were no different from those used in provincial schools were, therefore . . . particularly unsuitable. . . . Devoted teachers with imagination can make some use of them, [but] . . . in the hands of uninspired teachers they are deadly.' More importantly, the academic rigour and content of residential schools' curricula were compromised by the philosophies and morality of labour. The moral content of nebulous curricula was that moral redemption could not be found in books but could only happen through the learning of labour. At the turn of the century, the Department of Indian Affairs stated explicitly that the school program aimed to 'develop all the abilities, to remove prejudice against labour and give courage to compete with the rest of the world'(Miller, 1996: 155). In the next 30–40 years, the philosophies of hard work and moral education drove curricula to focus more and more on 'vocational education' that culminated in half-day schools in which formal education occurred for half a day and labour occupied the other half. Indeed, this educational regimen resulted in extracting free labour and not in imparting vocational learning. Egerton Ryerson's model of education for Indian communities was that the half-day system would eventually make schools self-sufficient and independent of public revenues (ibid.).

The entire system of 'miseducation' resulted in generations of Aboriginal children who were not only forcibly disconnected from their culture, but who also were relegated to educational failure. Research conducted in the 1980s (Barman et al., 1986) has shed light on the degree of educational failure. For example, between 1890 and 1950, depending on the decade, between 60 and 80 per cent of Aboriginal children in federal day and residential schools failed to advance past Grade 3. Further (ibid., 9), in 1930:

> three quarters of the Indian pupils across Canada were in grades 1 to 3, receiving only basic literary education. Only three in every hundred went past grade six. By comparison, well over half the children in provincial public schools in 1930 were past grade 3; almost a third were beyond grade six.

Clearly, the system of federal education of Aboriginal children was devoted to the continuing relegation of generations of Aboriginal people to the margins of society.

The claim has been made that modern-day schools are, in part, institutions of social placement and social reproduction in which implicit and explicit educational streaming of students leads ultimately to selected socio-economic strata. Certainly, the devastation wrought by residential and industrial schools left Aboriginal children socially marginalized or excluded. Helen Cote (2001: 56) describes how residential schooling contributed to socio-economic marginalization for a damaged people:

> We were not a threat to anyone. In that residential school we lived in fear. When we left that residential school, some of us promptly killed ourselves, or drowned our sorrows in drugs and alcohol. We went away to hide from our people, being too ashamed to look at them. Some of us died with our shame, therefore leaving our shame to be lived on in our children and grandchildren. The cycle continues because we have no money to improve our lives. They have taken our land, our powers and have killed our wills to live.

The residential school system not only reproduced the Indian as savage but resulted in an epidemic of socio-cultural devastation that, as Cote and others have argued, continues today.

THE MODERN LEGACY

The period of education that we have just described, which lasted, ostensibly, until the end of World War II, has been labelled, rather benignly, as the paternalistic phase. Until 1945, Native schooling was 'education in isolation'. During this period, schools and hostels for Indian children were established, but scant attention was paid to developing a curriculum geared to either their language difficulties or their sociological needs. A few Indian bands established schools for their children on the reserves, but the majority of them had neither the financial resources nor the leadership to establish and operate their own schools. Provincial governments were too preoccupied with their own priorities to become involved in Indian education. Missionaries provided a modicum of services, but their 'noble savage' philosophy effectively insulated the Indians from the mainstream of society (Special Senate Hearing on Poverty, 1970: 14, 59, quoted in Frideres, 1998: 150).

This official view of the history of residential schools as paternalistic stands in contrast to some of the works we have discussed in this chapter that describe a much more malevolent government bent on appropriating land by destroying the inhabitants of that land. This view is shared by observers such as Chrisjohn and Young (1997: 3), who argue quite strongly that:

> Residential schools were one of many attempts at the genocide of the Aboriginal Peoples inhabiting the area now commonly called Canada. Initially, the goal of obliterating these peoples was connected with stealing what they owned (the land, the sky, the waters, and their lives, all that these encompassed); and although this connection persists, present-day acts and policies of genocide are also connected with the hypocritical, legal, and self-delusional need on the part of the perpetrators to conceal what they did and what they continue to do.

The subsequent historical period, described euphemistically as the 'democratic ideology' (Frideres, 1998), was based on an 'open-door' policy in which Aboriginal children could attend schools off reserve. The impetus for this policy came from a realization that the cultural and personal destruction wrought by residential schools could no longer be tolerated or at least rationalized. However, the enduring belief in integration and assimilation still framed educational policy change. The 1967 Hawthorn Report, authored by anthropologist Harry B. Hawthorn, who was appointed by the federal government to conduct an inquiry into the economic, political, and educational needs of Canada's Native population, explored the underprivileged place of Aboriginal peoples in Canadian society. One of its central mandates was to assess the failure of education for Aboriginal people and to provide a framework for upward mobility for First Nations citizens. The philosophy that framed this project was decidedly assimilationist, with the enduring expectation that for First Nations people to become productive citizens they had to be schooled in the ways of industrial white society. Part of the rhetoric of this policy was that indigenous ways stood in the way of personal and social progress. Although couched in politically astute terminology, the discourse of public policy was framed around ethnocentric propositions that were hidden by a discourse of progress and mobility. The following excerpts from the Hawthorn Report (1967: 5–8) illustrate how government policy attempted to be culturally sensitive and somewhat self-reflective but really condemned First Nations culture in the process:

> The background of the stress on schooling and its results is interwoven with needs for better employment, better health and livelihood, more capital for enterprise and a greater share in the governmental and political life of Canada. . . . The fuller achievement of goals in many of these areas is ordinarily and obviously dependent on a certain level of schooling. . . . Indians must receive some wider responsibilities and a fuller place in Canadian life in order that learning can have enough meaning for their children. The child at school needs to see while he learns that an Indian can do other things besides logging, trapping, fishing or small farming.
>
> What the school wants the child to be like above all is the ideal middle-class Canadian child. At this point and in this study we do not propose to weigh the values of Indian childhood and the values of middle-class Canadian childhood and attempt to say which is better. . . . But since the Indian child often lacks a spokesman, and since later in the Report we comment unfavorably on aspects of his life which we think are harmful to him, we will note here that the qualities of independence,

self-reliance and non-competitiveness which he commonly brings to school are not negligible ones, and in some of the major countries of the world would fit him well for life. But these qualities do not fit as well in a contemporary Canadian school, and the child's lack of many items of knowledge possessed by the ordinary White child is very unfitting in that context.

Being an Indian has become an uncertain thing. The child entering school finds that out for the first time, and is offered no way to resolve the uncertainty. In some ways his situation is like that of children from many other minority families except that the other parents are likely to have insisted that their home values have an esteemed historical past, written down and accepted, and their children may soon grow to know that they can cite authority for speaking, acting and looking as their families do.

The questioning of Aboriginal people and culture lies in a discourse of difference. Aboriginal children, despite their admirable qualities of independence, self-reliance, and non-competitiveness, are not quite appropriate for Canadian schools/society. The authors of the report, despite the fact that they declared Aboriginal people to be 'citizens plus', maintained that teachers face considerable challenges in having Aboriginal children in their classrooms and that these teachers must 'continue to take refuge in the "rightness" of their ways and struggle onward in the task of "helping children overcome their Indianness"' (Hawthorn Report, 1967: 121). Quite clearly, the report implies that in order to partake of the Canadian way, the child must learn to abandon his/her native ways. Apparently 'logging, trapping, fishing and small farming' are inferior pursuits in the Canadian industrial model. We do not have to analyze any more deeply the language of the report to uncover a view that applauds the 'noble savage' child while maintaining that such a child is better placed with children from other cultures. Verna St Denis, a Canadian Aboriginal scholar, has recently produced a treatise on the Hawthorn Report and identifies the assimilationist nature of the document and how, despite its expressed good intentions, it was based on a body of knowledge that failed to incorporate the knowledges of Aboriginal people and focused on the 'psychology of Indian people'. St Denis argues that the report is a typical example of policy that blames the victim by focusing on the Indian psychology and the culture of Indian people as primarily responsible for educational failure (St Denis, 2002).

The final implication is a warning that, to survive, the Indian child and his/her family must adapt to the values and pursuits of the white Canadian world. The 'democratic phase' in Aboriginal education in Canada was, quite clearly, assimilationist more than it was democratic.

The historical reality is that, despite the general belief that the residential school program was largely a failure and that integration was consistent with national education policy, the residential school system persisted for four decades into this 'democratic' period. As Milloy argues, however, the residential schools changed from places of education to places of child care. This newly adopted welfare role was based on a rather general belief that '[t]heir parents would not be able to "assume responsibility for the care of their children," upon which integration/closure policy depended' (Milloy, 1999: 211). In fact, the rhetoric of public policy at the time was that Aboriginal parents were to be rated as to their worthiness to raise children, and their children were subsequently judged as to their welfare needs. The criteria for assessing neglect and worthiness, however, were strongly biased in favour of non-Aboriginal values based largely on the concept of the nuclear family. The characteristics that became part of the social service files of indicted families included 'father shiftless . . . unmarried mother . . . very large family . . . very poor home' (ibid., 213). Many of the traits of Aboriginal families in trouble were often connected to economic conditions and ultimately to the marginality of Aboriginal communities. However, the files of Aboriginal families that remained in the public archives were stories of impaired people. Milloy observes that '[t]he official view seemed to be that the need for welfare and residential placement was not a product of economic circumstances but of parental moral shortcomings' (ibid., 214). The grim result of all of this is that, in the 1960s and 1970s, upwards of 50 per cent of children in residential schools were there because they had been judged to be neglected and their families were assessed as inadequate. Obviously, the official judgments surrounding Aboriginal family morality had a strong class bias.

Ironically, the day school system that accompanied the persistent residential school system and that became a large part of Aboriginal education from the 1950s on still lacked adequate teachers and adequate curricula. As the Royal Commission on Aboriginal Peoples showed, despite efforts to attract more competent staff through competitive salaries and the abandonment of the half-day system, by the 1980s the Department of Indian Affairs had ongoing trouble recruiting and keeping teachers in both day and residential schools. In addition, as the Commission declared, 'both the curriculum and the pedagogy made it difficult for the children to learn . . . . Although the department admitted in the 1970s that the curriculum had not been geared to the children's sociological needs, it did little to rectify the situation' (Royal Commission on Aboriginal Peoples, 1996b: 345). While there was a growing body of evidence on culturally inoffensive teaching materials and on the impact that such material had on Aboriginal children, none of this research informed the decisions of educational policy-makers. The Royal Commission's summary statement on this matter (Royal Commission on Aboriginal Peoples, 1996c: 434) suggests without equivocation that current educational policy in Canada fails to meet the cultural, spiritual, and educational needs of Aboriginal children:

> The majority of Aboriginal youth do not complete high school. They leave the school system without the requisite skills for employment [and] without the language and cultural knowledge of their people. Rather than nurturing the individual, the school experience typically erodes identity and self-worth. Those who continue in Canada's formal education systems told us of regular encounters with racism, racism expressed not only in interpersonal exchanges but also through the denial of Aboriginal values, perspectives and cultures in the curriculum and the life of the institution.

Harold Cardinal (1977: 72) warned several decades ago that 'the problem here is simple but frightening. Children who are bused off to provincial schools very quickly wind up not being able to talk to their own parents.' Knockwood (1992: 156) describes how 'many had difficulties when they left school finding an identity and place in the world. . . . Some went home to the reserves after being discharged from the school only to find out that they didn't fit in.' They were not only jettisoned from white society but were treated often as outsiders in their home communities, especially when they attempted to criticize those communities based on their experiences on the outside: 'when they tried to point out the social ills at home, they were told "You don't belong here. Go back to where you came from." Even those of us who had parents who welcomed us home were suspended in limbo, because we could no longer speak Mi'kmaw' (ibid.).

In Chapter 4, we will hear the voices of Aboriginal students who are faced with the realities described above. In Chapter 6, we will provide examples of school systems that have responded in a caring and nurturing way to the damage wrought by over a century of mal-derived, mal-intentioned education for Aboriginal children.

THE LEGACY

The legacy of Aboriginal residential schools in Canada can be understood at both a simple and a complex level. The simple level involves understanding federal control of Aboriginal education as part of colonialist expansion and Canadian national policy of development and industrialization in which Aboriginal people and their cultures, existing in their current state, were posed as an impediment. Our intention in this chapter, however, has been to show that the history of Canadian Aboriginal education must be understood at a more complex level and that the interpretations of the history and the motives of a colonizing Euro-Canadian society are most profoundly presented through what has been described as 'standpoint epistemology'. This position suggests that the best and most valid interpretations of socio-historical events come from the oppressed, because they understand the lived reality of the oppressed. By presenting the works of survivors of residential schools within a broader political economic framework, we not only draw on their experiences to support our polemic, but we accept their insights as the most important reading of history. The legacy we present in the sections that follow is a composite of their stories and our critical reading of Canadian history.

DAMAGED GENERATIONS

First, and most importantly, generations of abuse by commission or omission in residential schools have left an infamous legacy for Aboriginal communities. Cote (2001) and Knockwood (1992) describe how their treatment has resulted in generations of damaged peoples. The writing of Helen Cote (2001) depicts how the enormous and ongoing involvement of Aboriginal people in the justice system can, in most cases, be linked to abuse in residential school. Her story is one of how physical and emotional torture not only damages the spirit, but also distorts the world view to a point at which the damaged spirit will do anything to escape the horror of the past. She, her parents, and her siblings escaped into a world of substance abuse that literally killed many of them. Knockwood reveals, on the other hand, how abuse in residential schools instilled a fear of touching in the survivors to the point where they hated to show physical affection. The most devastating effect of this was borne out in parenting practices described by a woman survivor:

> Today I have a hard time, I don't want anybody to touch me unless I'm really close to them. I even have a hard time shaking hands. I want to be close to my family, but they're like me, afraid to hug me. The closest thing they ever tell me is, 'See you tomorrow.' (Knockwood, 1992: 157)

Her mother also had been a student at the school and she writes of how her mother's reticence to talk resulted from experiences in school.

THE DESTRUCTION OF CULTURE AND SPIRITUALITY

'Those who ran the school tried to rob us of our collective identity by punishing us for speaking our language, calling us "savages" and "heathens"' (ibid.). Through the direct attack on culture and spirituality, the residential school system created children and youth who were welcome in neither Aboriginal nor white cultures. When children returned home and criticized the home community, they were, at worst, shunned as outsiders or, at best, left in limbo as their new experiences and new language made them foreigners. The Royal Commission on Aboriginal Peoples (1996c: 374), in reference to a small group of former 'successful' residential school students whose opinions were canvassed by the Department of Indian Affairs in the 1960s, noted that '[t]he former students consulted in 1965 were unanimous in the opinion that for most children, the school experience was "really detrimental to the development of the human being". Isolated from both the Aboriginal and non-Aboriginal community, schools were "inclined to make robots of their students", who were quite incapable of facing "a world almost unknown to them".'

EDUCATION AS A CLASS WEAPON

We commented earlier in this chapter that the Canadian state, through the Department of Indian Affairs, created dossiers on Indian families and assessed children into categories of appropriateness for school. These files, in large part, were based on evidence about the level of privation in which the family (or the community) lived and the discourse about child welfare became a language of indictment of poverty. In the end, families and children became identified and blamed for being poor. The culture of poverty mentality that framed government and church thinking drew on education to create a self-fulfilling prophecy whereby poor children from poor families could not possibly succeed in educational institutions built upon middle-class parochial values and temporal demands. Chrisjohn and Young (1997: 62–3) argue that:

> 'Limited' education has been a policy of European religious institutions long before Columbus, the tactic serving in earlier eras to establish and maintain the within-society colonisation known as class through obfuscations such as the 'doctrines' of Innate Depravity, Original Sin, and the Divine Right of Kings, and the promise of 'something better' in the 'next' world. This long history of the use of education as a weapon of oppression has largely been concealed, and though sometimes barbed with religion, sometimes predominantly secular, the weapon was, as was the case with Indian Residential Schooling, generally fashioned cooperatively by church and state. This 'moralistic camouflage' has served both to isolate historically the aims and achievements of Indian Residential Schooling (thus contributing to its systematic misunderstanding), and to prevent the various victims of this strategy from comparing notes and making common cause.

THE PATHOLOGY OF OPPRESSION

In the 1950s and 1960s, as the Canadian state searched its collective soul for answers to the 'problem of Indian education', much of the rhetoric of change and improvement involved the quest to pathologize the effects of residential schooling. The 'Residential School Syndrome' (Chrisjohn and Young, 1997) became the mantra of a society hoping to gain political absolution by treating its victims as sick and in need of care and therapy. As determined by many institutions concerned with issues of medicine and deviance, the sick person needs to accept the sick role before he or she is deemed worthy of therapy. This was the case for many survivors of residential school who readily took part in psychotherapy as part of the solution. While the efficacy of psychotherapy is not in question here, the state's role in promoting a sickness model as the starting point for resolution is. The syndrome mentality shuts down other avenues of explanation; it prevents us, at least at the political level, from considering more structural/political sources of damage and victimization and, as Chrisjohn and Young (ibid., 80–1) state, 'The meaning of Indian

Residential Schooling is not the pathology it may have created in some Aboriginal peoples; it is the pathology it reveals in the "system of order" giving rise to it.'

THE DEFAMATION OF CHILDREN

The final legacy of the residential school period is the most difficult to chronicle and, yet, is likely the most traumatic for all cultures. In Aboriginal societies, children are regarded as a precious gift and are central to their world view. The reasoning behind this is simple—the destiny of a culture is closely bound to the welfare of its young. Education, of course, is inextricably bound to the welfare of children and youth, especially insofar as it prepares for life and not just work. Traditional Aboriginal philosophies of education were based on the assumption that education is lifelong and that teaching should prepare young people to participate fully in the spiritual, cultural, physical, and emotional life of the society. In an educational context like this, the concepts of 'failure' and 'pass' are irrelevant. In fact, the competitiveness of conventional education is anathema to learning. In this light, then, what the residential school experience did was to reroute Aboriginal children from a true apprenticeship for living to a false apprenticeship for democratic and labour force participation. One of the tragedies of this transformation is that the costs of failure are immense and Aboriginal children were consigned to failure. In final analysis, the combination of failure and abuse led to a massive devaluation of children from their accustomed place in cultural life. This devaluation was especially acute in the eyes of the children themselves. They have been removed from a place of privilege and care to a place of defamation and abuse.

QUESTIONS FOR CRITICAL THOUGHT

1. In what two ways are survivors of Aboriginal residential schools making their voices heard? Why is it important to draw from survivors' personal accounts?
2. What have been the main consequences of the imposition of Euro-Canadian models of education on Canada's Aboriginal peoples? How do these experiences compare with instances of colonial control in other nations?
3. Why was residential schooling introduced by the Canadian government? What benefits did it offer the Canadian state and economic system? What arguments did the government use to justify church involvement in operating

residential schools? How did religious involvement affect the curriculum, content, and organization of these schools?

4. Compare and contrast the treatment of Aboriginal children in residential schools with the treatment of immigrants and non-Aboriginal orphans during the same period in Canadian history.

5. How did the system of schooling for Aboriginal children change following the Hawthorn Report? What consequences did these developments have for Aboriginal students and their families?

6. Discuss the significance of notions of healing for residential school survivors and Aboriginal communities. What kinds of strategies should be employed by governments and Aboriginal communities to accomplish objectives of healing?

RECOMMENDED READING

Dickason, Olive Patricia. 2001. *Canada's First Nations: A History of Founding Peoples from Earliest Times*, 3rd edn. Toronto: Oxford University Press.

> The author presents a sweeping historical record of Aboriginal peoples in Canada from the original peopling and settlement of the Americas to first contacts with Europeans and other non-Aboriginals, through the European settlement and industrialization of Canada, to the modern era characterized by issues of self-government and the settlement of land claims agreements. Dickason's work is important reading for those interested in understanding Canadian history and the significant and continuing role Canada's founding peoples have played in this country's settlement, development, culture, and politics.

Jaine, Linda. 1993. *Residential School: The Stolen Years*. Saskatoon: University Extension Press.

> This work presents the stories of indigenous people who attended residential schools. These first-hand accounts help us to understand how an oppressive education system imposed on First Nations children was both dehumanizing and counterproductive. The narratives are not so much shocking as they are disheartening, especially because religion and education are proclaimed to be fundamental and important institutions for social betterment.

Knockwood, Isabelle. 1992. *Out of the Depths: The Experience of Mi'kmaw Children at the Indian Residential School at Shubenacadie*. Lockeport, NS: Roseway Publishing.

Based on interviews with survivors of abuse in an Indian residential school in Nova Scotia, *Out of the Depths* presents heart-rending accounts of the abject exploitation of First Nations children by those who were charged to protect and teach them. The stories show clearly how indigenous children were trapped in a system that exploited their labour, diminished their culture, and threatened their physical and emotional health under the guise of 'bringing Indians into the twentieth century'.

Miller, J.R. 1996. *Shingwauk's Vision: A History of Native Residential Schools.* Toronto: University of Toronto Press.

This book surveys the history of Indian residential schools in Canada from the early seventeenth century in New France and covers the colonial period, the creation of residential schools late in the nineteenth century, and finally the phasing out of the government-sponsored schools in the 1960s. Miller uncovers and discusses the motives and practices of government and religious administrators towards First Nations peoples. *Shingwauk's Vision* is an excellent historical reference based on archival research and interviews with Native peoples.

Milloy, John S. 1999. *A National Crime: The Canadian Government and the Residential School System, 1879–1986.* Winnipeg: University of Manitoba Press.

Milloy's thorough study is perhaps the most daring and well-chronicled expression of the calculated and protracted abuse of Aboriginal children in Indian residential schools. It is both historically rich and daringly insightful.

❖

CHAPTER 4

THE VOICES OF STUDENTS OF ABORIGINAL ANCESTRY

INTRODUCTION

We have observed that Aboriginal people regard education as integral to their efforts to regain their identity and establish an equitable footing in Canadian society. However, encouraging initiatives and improved educational participation and performance are offset by evidence that progress towards educational and socio-economic equity has not matched expectations. The need to assess prospects for improved educational success among First Nations and Métis students in Canada is especially significant considering the increasing proportion of Aboriginal people in Canada, their projected labour force needs, the importance of education for future social and economic development, and the importance of redressing historical wrongs. This chapter examines one particular dimension of these issues that has rarely been addressed in previous research—Aboriginal students' own accounts of their educational experiences and aspirations.

Previous research and policy analysis have pointed to the interactions among in-school factors, educational governance and resources, and community factors as determinants of potential educational success among Aboriginal students (Royal Commission on Aboriginal Peoples, 1996b; Satzewich and Wotherspoon, 2000). Within schools, educational success is associated with teachers, curricula, and practices that incorporate knowledge and understanding of Aboriginal culture together with empathy for Aboriginal students. Conversely, features of schooling that ignore the needs of the Aboriginal learner, or operate with the consciousness of a gap between cultures uppermost in values and goals, tend to reduce educational performance, often leading to failure or dropout. This reality was no more evident than in the residential schools described in Chapter 3, through which education played both direct and indirect roles in devastating the potential of generations of Aboriginal students. Clearly, this history and the current state of Aboriginal educational attainment in Canada show that improved educational performance requires meaningful educational participation by Aboriginal people, and resource support built upon active involvement and commitment to positive educational development. The achievement of educational success also requires that the analysis of school policy take into account the concerns and experiences that all educational participants bring with them into the school and the distinct community, political, and socio-economic environments in which the schools are situated.

RATIONALE FOR THE STUDY

Saskatchewan has, with Manitoba, the highest concentration of Aboriginal people among Canadian provinces, estimated in 1996 to be 11.4 per cent of the total population with a projected growth to 13.9 per cent or higher by 2016 (Statistics Canada, 1998a; Royal Commission on Aboriginal Peoples, 1996b: 22). The proportion of children of First Nations and Métis ancestry, which constituted 18 per cent of the total provincial school population in 1991, is expected to grow to about 30 per cent by 2006 (Saskatchewan Education, 1991: 5). It is projected that, among registered Indians alone, current levels of entry into the province's labour force (an estimated 1,500 to 2,000 young people annually) will continue at least through the next decade (Working Margins Consulting Group, 1992: 5).

The changing demographic constitution of the province's population requires growing sensitivity to several important sets of factors. Foremost among these are demands for educational programming and services that will meet the diverse needs of pupils who are in or will soon be moving through the school system and, second, public expectations that students will be adequately prepared for post-school transition processes into the labour force or continuing or post-secondary educational institutions.

The evidence to date suggests that, while a great deal more needs to be known about how those demographic and transition processes operate, Saskatchewan schools, like those in other parts of Canada, are doing a mixed job of retaining and training Aboriginal children and youth. On the one hand, more First Nations and Métis pupils than ever before are enrolled in school and staying longer. Nationally, in 1996, 81.6 per cent of the on-reserve registered First Nations school-age population were attending school full-time, about three-quarters of pupils were staying in

school continuously to the end of grade 12, and post-secondary enrolment rates had doubled over the previous decade (Department of Indian
Affairs and Northern Development Canada, 1997: 33–7). In all of these
regards, long-standing gaps between Aboriginal and non-Aboriginal populations remained, but they had declined from previous levels.
Nonetheless, dropout rates have continued to be high, and educational
achievements have remained well below levels that observers consider to
be satisfactory (Gabriel Dumont Institute, 1993; Saskatchewan Treaty
Indians, 1993; Mills Consulting, 1993). By the end of the 1990s, enrolments of registered Indians at elementary, secondary, and post-secondary
levels had levelled off or even declined (Department of Indian Affairs and
Northern Development Canada, 2000: 28–9). The Federation of
Saskatchewan Indian Nations (1997: 87), as we have already noted, cites
the lower than average educational attainments by Aboriginal people in
the province as a contributing factor to an 'Aboriginal economic gap'
characterized by unemployment, income deficiencies, and underutilized
productivity; and there is an insufficient pool of qualified workers for
highly skilled and professional occupations (see also Working Margins
Consulting Group, 1992: 50).

Consequently, several organizations have called for systematic
research that will enable us to examine how educational processes currently operate for Aboriginal people in such a way as to either facilitate or
restrict their educational progress. The Saskatchewan Aboriginal
Education Provincial Advisory Committee (initially constituted as the
Saskatchewan Indian and Métis Education Advisory Committee in order
to recommend actions to the provincial education ministry to improve
education for Aboriginal people) has advocated since 1984 a series of
action plans intended to foster participation, curricular content, and
organizational practices that will make the school system more supportive and conducive to success for Aboriginal people (Saskatchewan
Education, 1991), while the Saskatchewan Treaty Indians (1993: 7) have
stressed the need for research and for 'better, more integrated data systems to understand First Nations participation in education within a total
demographic context'.

The research project outlined in this chapter is one of several projects
sponsored by Saskatchewan Education in response to a series of research
priorities identified by the Saskatchewan Indian and Métis Education
Research Network. It is sensitive to the view, expressed by Ovide
Mercredi, formerly the National Chief of the Assembly of First Nations,

and reiterated by many others in the context of the federal Royal Commission on Aboriginal Peoples, that 'Native people have been studied to death.' At the same time, a pressing need continues for meaningful research that can incorporate the voices of Aboriginal community members in such a way as to contribute to effective social and economic change.

THE RESEARCH METHOD

Part 1: The Purpose of the Study

The project addresses the roles, perceptions, and experiences of Aboriginal students in four atypical Saskatchewan schools in relation to expectations and practices that occur both in and outside of school settings. The study has been organized in such a way as to give voice to First Nations and Métis students to determine how they assess their educational experiences and how these perceptions are related to other aspects of their lives and to their expectations about their futures. Motivated by an Aboriginal perspective, the study adopts a holistic perspective, which views education as an integral part of broader social experience.

The research focuses on three main questions:

1. What factors do First Nations and Métis students identify as the strengths and limitations of their schooling?
2. How relevant is schooling, according to the perceptions of First Nations and Métis students, to their out-of-school experiences and aspirations?
3. What is the relationship between these student perceptions and various social factors in and out of school?

In order to address these questions, research was conducted in 1997 and 1998 in the form of talking circles involving First Nations and Métis students in selected elementary and secondary schools in Saskatchewan, and interviews were arranged and held with a sub-sample of students in those groups. Each of the schools has developed unique programs favouring Aboriginal youth. Each of the schools represents a different sort of tie with the local school board. The quantitative data are based on interviews with 65 elementary students in a conventional school and 25 high school students in alternative schools in northern Saskatchewan and in

Saskatoon, described more fully below. The three talking circles were conducted at an alternative high school in Prince Albert and represented the contributions of 32 students, all of whom were Aboriginal—one of these was an Inuk. The latter high school has approximately 50 students enrolled full-time.

Part 2: The Subjects: The Four Schools and the Students

Princess Alexandria School in Saskatoon is a community-based public elementary school in the inner city where the population is relatively poor and more transient than average. Both the school and the community deal with day-to-day issues that are characteristic of communities functioning on the margins of society. Many of the parents in the community are struggling economically and personally and, as a result, some students are disadvantaged and in need when they enter school. The school works closely with the local community association and with community groups and agencies to access resources for students and parents.

The school has responded to the issues that students face in the following ways:

1. The school has abandoned punishment as a disciplinary option and replaced it with a system of reparation and responsibility. To this end, the staff are prepared to accept that 'acting out' and verbal abuse will occur, knowing that these behaviours arise from traumatic life experiences. Because the staff at the school either self-select or are handpicked, they are aware the children require exceptional nurturing.

2. Standardized education presents a problem for alternative schools like Princess Alexandria because it is not designed for the distinctive needs of the students. Princess Alexandria School has responded by creating a flexible curriculum in which the students are assessed on the basis of individual progress and success. The school program clusters students according to academic and social needs rather than grouping them in single-grade classrooms, and the school has an alternative school day that involves a shifting of the school hours to a later start time with a more limited lunch break.

3. This essentially human rights approach to education (Schissel, 1997) involves an understanding not only of the emotional needs of the students but also of their immediate physical and economic needs. The school responds, with the help of the community, by providing break-

fast and lunch programs and by providing 'work for wages' opportunities around the school for the older children. Furthermore, the school attempts to create a physical environment that is safe and secure. Recesses are replaced with two periods of physical education to keep students 'off the street'. The schoolyard is maintained by custodial staff who are involved in environmental programs that include students designing and maintaining the school property. This caretaker involvement is rather unique in that it draws on caretakers from the local community who volunteer their time on weekends to teach ecology classes to students and maintain the schoolyard with student help. This example, in particular, illustrates how the school and local community members come together to create an educational environment that works and extends beyond the classrooms.

4. In 2001, over 95 per cent of the 250 students in the pre-kindergarten to grade 8 school were of Aboriginal ancestry. Consequently, the school, because it is comprised primarily of students of Aboriginal ancestry and visible minority students, incorporates cultural traditions into its curriculum, including Native dance, spirituality, and art and cross-cultural learning. Issues of trauma and sexuality are addressed in a very direct and non-accusatory way. When dealing with issues of physical and sexual abuse, the school meets as a community of children and adults to respond to such issues more generally. For example, when one 11-year-old girl had been sexually assaulted outside the school, the teachers, all the children, a social worker, and an Elder all met to discuss issues of assault and abuse and to destigmatize the victim. The overall purpose of such activity is to deal with specific traumatic incidents by placing them in the context of general issues of safety and security and, in so doing, allowing the trauma of the victim to be shared by the community. These efforts permit the student to return to school in an atmosphere of understanding and not of pity and fear.

5. The school also deals with issues of sexuality and sexually transmitted diseases in the same community context. Such issues are dealt with as larger social issues that involve safety, mutual respect, issues of safe sex at a general level, and respect for gender. The morality of blame is not part of the discussion (Schissel, 1997). Issues of gender, sex, and sexuality, which are often ignored or discussed in a circumspect fashion in conventional school systems, are dealt with directly as public issues of collective concern.

In the end, the success of the school is indicated by high attendance, punctuality, positive feedback from parents and students, increased job satisfaction for teachers, 60 per cent fewer incidents of youth misconduct in the community than before the community school was formed, and almost no incidents of students leaving during the day. The success of the school is attributable to (1) staff who have taken on responsibilities beyond their traditional role (including a willingness to tolerate and understand difference and defiance), (2) community volunteers (from a hospital and local retail store, for example), and (3) a police force that has participated in a police liaison project within the school. Ultimately, these caring adults are willing and prepared to construct an alternative learning context for young people.

Won Ska Cultural School in Prince Albert, Saskatchewan, demonstrates the potential for an integrated community-based school and the obstacles that prevent it from becoming an acceptable framework for public education, especially for children and youth who live on the margins of society. Won Ska teaches First Nations street kids and adults who generally have been in trouble with the law, that is, students who are identified by social services as 'at risk'. The school was started in 1993 in response to a high dropout rate for Aboriginal students in Prince Albert. First Nations and Métis parents, community agency workers, teachers from other schools who had a vision for a new school, and local youth created a template for the school, which was originally funded by Saskatchewan Education and now operates within the Prince Albert school district.

Several things are remarkable about the school with respect to the effectiveness with which it is filling the needs of its students. First, for many of the students who have been in trouble with the law, school is the only place where they can deal with the issues that resulted in their legal problems. It provides opportunities for the students to talk about their personal problems, not only to engage in academic programs. Second, schools that help students deal with the transition from childhood/adolescence to adulthood as a fundamental priority provide a better learning environment in all subject areas, and Won Ska meets that fundamental priority. This school is administered in a democratic context in which students have the final say in the educational development. To this end, the teacher as mentor is of deep importance; the principal, with the support of the school board, hand-picks certified teachers who have a commitment to alternative educational models, which includes not only training and the transmission of knowledge, but also the creation of a mutual, idea-sharing context in which the mentor is prepared to listen as much as s/he speaks. Many of the marginalized students in this school have missed out on the fundamental rights of children, which include: a concerned and tolerant audience; a physically and emotionally safe place to learn; a place where what they say is as important as what they hear; a chance to influence their life circumstances; an opportunity to make explanation and reparation; and a chance to see and emulate responsible, continually present and engaged adults.

The students' need for adult models frames this paradigm of learning. It is through interaction with and emulation of caring adults that marginalized youth develop basic life skills: to do the day-to-day tasks that facilitate living, to understand what constitutes responsible parenting and responsible intimacy, to overcome the frustration that lands them in trouble, to practise self-control, and to learn to trust people in positions of authority. The majority of students in alternative educational programs (students who are mostly from the streets or who are in young offender alternative measures programs), whom we have interviewed, have expressed an overwhelming fear and distrust of police and other legal officials and a generalized discomfort in conventional schools. Many of these students, when asked where they would be without an effective alternative school, immediately responded that they would likely be in jail.

By using education to teach academics, life skills, and self-empowerment, the school is able to take the negative legal experiences of its students and develop a system of healing that focuses on healthy, non-offending lifestyles. Thus, Won Ska provides an important antidote to the stigma of at-risk designations. The teachers also focus, almost exclusively, on the future and essentially ignore the histories of their students. In so doing, they eliminate labels such as 'at risk', 'young offender', or 'high needs'. Instead, they focus on what the students need to develop intellectually and socially. This policy of discarding labels is very much in accord with First Nations spirituality and healing, which eliminates guilt and blame from the healing process. At a very basic level, the concept of 'at risk' has an element of blame attached to it. Importantly, an education-based approach to youth justice does not preclude the courts and the police. On the contrary, it asks that policing and jurisprudence expand to incorporate issues of social justice, social and personal health, and preventive social reform. In short, the schools, in concert with the legal systems, become places where high-risk children, youths, and adults learn not only educational and occupational skills (and meaningful appren-ticeship) but also the skills for meaningful citizenship.

In addition, the school operates on the basis of consensus, with top-down authority minimized to the point that students decide on curricu-lum, marking, school social events, and aspects of school administration, all of which are imposed in traditional systems. The rationale for doing this is that a basic problem for marginal youth is their disenfranchised position in the world. By investing their lives with volition, the school seeks to demonstrate to students that, despite the labels that have been placed on them, their present role is one of importance and credibility. The result is that the retention rates within the school are high; when stu-dents discussed their educational satisfaction, their main comments focused on their wish to stay at school 24 hours a day.

The basic problem for Won Ska School, despite its record of success with educationally and socially damaged students, is that it is constantly fighting for enough physical and financial resources to provide a com-fortable school. And it is continually fighting for credibility. The school's approach poses several problems for the local school board. It defies a standard curriculum and replaces it with a student-driven program. It insists on a mentoring model of learning that often involves one-to-one learning, which is expensive. It ignores the offender/risk label of the stu-dents and refuses to engage in dialogue with the school board and the community when it is focused on 'high-risk', potentially dangerous stu-dents. Lastly, it allows students to remain in school as long as they wish, some well into their twenties, and this violates the traditional education-al focus on high school as a place only for adolescents.

Nutana Composite High School in Saskatoon provides another exam-ple of a clearly defined program for youth in trouble. Constituted as a community school that draws on the services of health, law, social servic-es, and community organizations, between 50 and 70 per cent of the stu-dent body are clients of social services at any one time. Eighty per cent of the students in Nutana are designated by the courts and social services as 'at-risk'. The school addresses the problems of these socially stigmatized students in several ways. It structures the needs of the students as indi-vidually as possible within a standardized curriculum. These needs are dictated by the students and are dependent on their life situations. For example, Nutana has a program for single mothers. While this program offers important educational opportunities for mothers and a daycare for children, it also provides a context in which the fathers can be involved

with their children, in short, a school atmosphere in which being preg-
nant or having a baby at a young age is not stigmatized. The school creates a climate in which being a young mother (or father) does not place
the baby at risk and that does not have to impair the educational and
social development of the mother or father. The school also tries to incorporate students and former students into the teaching process as student
aides, as facilitators in different types of self-help discussion groups, as
potential future teachers, and in youth leadership roles. This program is
successful, above and beyond the obvious learning and support advan-
tages it offers, because students who were once labelled 'at-risk' become
mentors and role models. Their stigma of 'being diagnosed' is replaced
with the honour of being respected. Nutana works very hard at dimin-
ishing at-risk designations by providing the students a context in which
they feel valuable and in which the public sees students as productive and
influential. Nutana's policy of using community resource people as much
as possible provides the opportunity for youth designated 'at-risk' to
interact with mainstream adults as real people, an important accomplishment in reframing the socio-legal discourse of offender/risk.

  Meadow Lake Community School Council, in the community of
Meadow Lake in northern Saskatchewan, incorporates democracy as the
bedrock of teaching, learning, and social healing. The community is
devoted to bridging the divide between Aboriginal and non-Aboriginal
peoples and has dedicated its educational policy to this goal. The first step
in this regard is an agreement between the Flying Dust First Nation and
the Meadow Lake Public School Division to build a new composite high
school funded by both jurisdictions and to establish a Community School
Governance Model to oversee the establishment of a new educational
model for the community. This governance agreement is the first of its
kind in Canada. Second, the education model they propose is based on an
annual survey of children and youth in the Meadow Lake community.
The survey investigates experiences with school, the law, substance use,
recreation, social interaction, high-risk behaviour, victimization, sexual
activity, financial need, diet and eating habits, and family. As a result of
the responses to this survey, the Community Youth Committee
suggests and helps implement policies that respond to areas of need
identified by the survey. To date, after the initial survey, the Community
Youth Committee, along with the Community School Council, has
helped establish several important initiatives in all the schools in the
community, including:

- hiring a full-time Cree teacher; Cree is available to students from grades 6 to 12;
- hiring three Native grandmothers to work in the junior schools;
- a nutrition program for all elementary students;
- a Pow Wow club for high school and junior high students;
- a recreation program for kindergarten to grade 5 students after school and coached by high school students, with parental supervision;
- intercultural evenings at which grandparents share their life experiences with the students;
- an Elders program in which Elders spend time in all the schools as learning resources for the teachers. The Elders have initially been involved in establishing 'talking circles' in each high school;
- a community kitchen where parents prepare nutritious meals to be taken home, if need be;
- literacy programs in schools and in the community;
- a re-entry program for students in grades 8 to 12;
- a summer program staffed by university students supported by parents and volunteers in delivering recreation, literacy, computer skills, and leisure activities.

As one reads through this litany of programs at Meadow Lake, it is important to understand that the specific needs addressed by these programs have been identified by the students themselves through what is planned to be an annual survey. Essentially, the commitment to a better community is made possible by the democratic initiative of the annual student survey. The way the community responds is based primarily on those needs voiced by the students. The school, in effect, becomes the vehicle for democratic participation by children and youth.

Part 3: Data Collection from Student Interviews

This research is based on interviews and talking circles with both elementary and secondary students of Aboriginal ancestry in the province of Saskatchewan. The data are based on transcripts of talking circles and interviews conducted in both rural and urban areas in conventional elementary schools and alternative high schools under provincial jurisdiction. Given the mandate of this research program, band-controlled and community schools are not part of the research.

The students interviewed were in classes of both Aboriginal and non-Aboriginal students, and Aboriginal students were taken out of their classes for the interviews and talking circles. The data focus on:

1. the cultural and educational context of the lives of the students;
2. the students' perceptions of their school experiences and their understandings of a better school system;
3. students' educational aspirations;
4. the effect of cultural education on educational outcomes.

The tables and figures in this chapter are derived from the interviews and are based on information categorized from the transcripts incorporating themes identified in the literature review but open to additional areas of insight provided by the students. We present discrete groupings of data, first for elementary and then for high school students, to give the reader some sense of how attitudes and orientations towards education may change across age and school systems. The quantitative data are based on interviews with 65 elementary students (in grades 3 and 6) from three conventional schools comprised of both Aboriginal and non-Aboriginal students and with 25 high school students in three alternative schools in northern Saskatchewan and in Saskatoon. Descriptions of the schools and the procedures for carrying out the research are provided in Appendix A. The interviews took approximately one hour and were based on both closed and open-ended questions (Appendix B). The alternative high schools are both run under the auspices of public school boards and their students are largely those who have been unsuccessful in conventional schools. In the Prince Albert school, the majority of students have been in trouble with the law at one time or another. The alternative school in Prince Albert is comprised exclusively of students of Aboriginal ancestry and approximately 60 per cent of the students at the school in Saskatoon are Aboriginal.

The three talking circles were conducted at the Alternative High School in Prince Albert and represented the voluntary contributions of 32 students, all of whom were Aboriginal—one of these was an Inuk. The high school has approximately 50 students enrolled full-time. The talking circles were conducted in conformity with cultural tradition; both research associates were of Aboriginal ancestry and have had experience with this tradition. The discussions from the talking circles were taped and the tapes were transcribed verbatim.

FINDINGS

Cultural and Educational Context

The first set of figures describes the cultural context in which students live. We focus here on issues of ancestry and language to help contextualize the cultural needs of the student respondents.

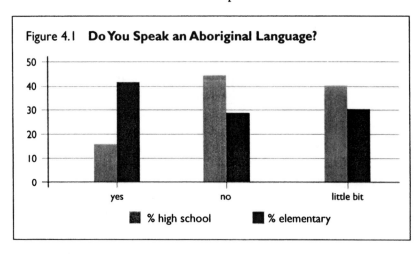

Figure 4.1   **Do You Speak an Aboriginal Language?**

Figure 4.1 indicates the prevalence of spoken Aboriginal languages among these students. High school students report considerably lower levels of spoken Aboriginal language (17 per cent) compared to elementary students, 40 per cent of whom report being bilingual. Over 40 per cent of the high school students do not speak an Aboriginal language at all compared to less than 30 per cent of the elementary students. It is possible that we are seeing a generational phenomenon here in which ancestral language is becoming more important to Aboriginal people as they strive for identity and self-determination. Younger students are possibly deriving the benefits of this growing cultural focus more so than older students. Nonetheless, considering students of all ages, it is clear that a majority of all students speak an ancestral language, at least to some degree.

As a further indication of the importance and prevalence of language and culture, 82 per cent of the elementary students and 100 per cent of high school students indicated that an Aboriginal language was spoken at home by family members. The talking circles corroborated the importance of language. All students agreed that their native tongue should be recognized as their first language and that they should be credited as being bilingual inside and outside school. The students in general saw the advantage of being bilingual as they felt that a Native language would allow them to work in a broad range of occupations related to Aboriginal people and that occupations based on traditional language use would permit the creation of more jobs for Aboriginal people, especially in the areas of health care, policing, and justice.

To get a sense of the educational cultural context for the Aboriginal students in our research, we asked about the number of Aboriginal teachers in the schools, and whether students like or dislike school in general.

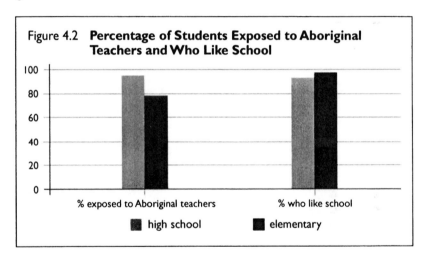

Figure 4.2   **Percentage of Students Exposed to Aboriginal Teachers and Who Like School**

This figure indicates that high percentages of all of the students are exposed to at least some Aboriginal teachers. On the other hand, it is noteworthy that for elementary students, 20 per cent do not have any Aboriginal teachers. It is clear that at both levels, the vast majority of students like school, which is reason for considerable optimism.

To explore the degree to which students have access in school to information about their own culture, we asked the elementary students whether culture is taught in school. Figure 4.3 shows that about 31 per cent said that culture is taught, 27 per cent responded 'never', while 19 per cent responded 'some'. Smaller percentages indicated that cultural teachings are limited to specific culture days or only in Native studies classes.

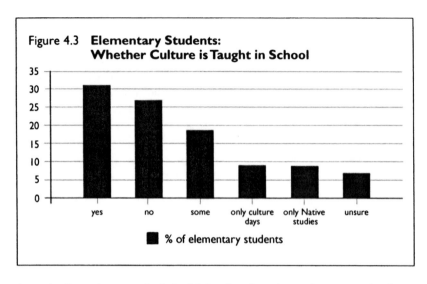

Figure 4.3   **Elementary Students:**
Whether Culture is Taught in School

In a similar vein, we asked the high school students the types of cultural education that they were offered in the alternative high schools (Figure 4.4).

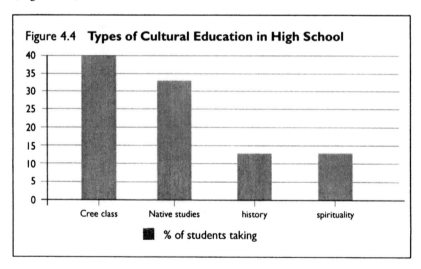

Figure 4.4   **Types of Cultural Education in High School**

Clearly, a substantial proportion of all students are exposed to Cree language class, Native studies classes, Aboriginal history, and spirituality classes.

We then asked the students to tell us the most important dimensions

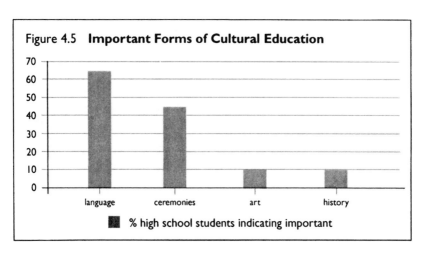

Figure 4.5   **Important Forms of Cultural Education**

% high school students indicating important

of cultural education. The totals in Figure 4.5 demonstrate that language is central to the cultural and educational needs of these high school students, with 65 per cent indicating its importance. The teaching of ceremonies (as noted by 45 per cent) is also substantially important. Of less importance are classes in art and history. Overall, however, students express a substantial desire for the teaching of language and ceremonies over and above what they are currently receiving.

The dialogue in the talking circles was very pointed with regard to cultural sensitivity and teaching. The students were unanimous in their conviction that Elders need to teach cultural training and Native studies. The students lament that non-Aboriginal teachers teach Native studies classes and that, despite their good intentions, the classes are delivered as academic subjects rather than profound cultural training. To this end, the students felt that greater involvement by Aboriginal people on school boards would facilitate greater involvement of Elders and other community members in the school. Conventional school boards are normally resistant to using formally 'unqualified' adults in school, and this appears to be a fundamental problem for the Aboriginal students we interviewed. Interestingly, administrators in two of the alternative schools that we investigated spent considerable amounts of time and energy defending, to their school boards, the credibility and success of their programs because of the unconventional nature of their curricula (generally determined by the students in consultation with staff), the predominance of one-to-one instruction, and the use of non-teacher community members (typically Elders).

Student Perception of School Experience

The first set of graphs presents important findings on students' understanding of what constitutes adequate and relevant education. Figures 4.6a and 4.6b illustrate what students perceive as barriers to their learning.

Racism is a problem for Aboriginal students, especially among those in high school. More than 35 per cent of the high school students rate this as

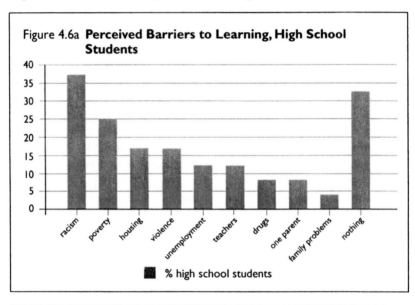

Figure 4.6a Perceived Barriers to Learning, High School Students

% high school students

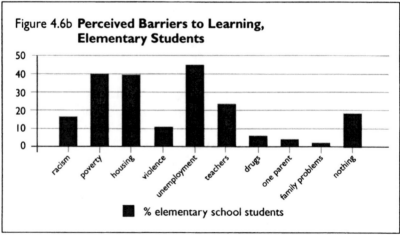

Figure 4.6b Perceived Barriers to Learning, Elementary Students

% elementary school students

the greatest barrier to learning. One high school student stated, for example, that the main barrier to learning for him and other Aboriginal students is 'prejudice, people calling us dumb First Nations and it sticks with us mentally.' Another student talked about a particular intolerant teacher as the main reason she disliked being in school: 'one was racist to me really bad, everybody knows that, all, like everyone there knows that this teacher is racist against all Natives—because she's home-ec. teacher. Like one out of four Native students would actually pass.' One high school student related a particularly poignant experience from his first year of school:

> My first day of kindergarten, I walked in to class, all the kids, it was story time, they moved to the other side of the room when I sat down, all the kids are on that side, and I'm thinking I didn't know the difference between white and Native—what is wrong with me? I went home and told my mom and that when she told me that I was Aboriginal, and I was like, 'What is that?' It was hard.

Another student expressed a dimension of discrimination that is rarely addressed in school policy and often overlooked in general discussions of students' well-being. She is a single mother with two children and her parenthood presents additional problems as a parent and as an Aboriginal young person:

> When I was young, I encountered a lot of racism, but that was dealing with colours, skin colours and hair colours, but now I think that what is racist or prejudiced, is, you see, a lot of young parents—there is racism towards those individuals. When you see an older couple, they look at you kinda weird, like you have two kids? Some people, my girlfriend was in Superstore one time buying groceries with her son and this couple said, 'Are you babysitting?' Some people are just rude, and it really brings a person's self-esteem down.

Discrimination on the basis of race and youth and parenthood is often overlooked in schools. If schools have programs for single parents, the practical needs of being a parent and being a student are given priority over academic expediency to help students buffer the anxiety and animosity of a rather moralistic, orthodox society. Incidentally, young mothers bear the brunt of such animosity, much more so than young fathers.

Racism appears to be less of a barrier for elementary students, who rate parental unemployment, housing, poverty, and hunger as more important concerns. It is noteworthy that high school students, too, rank socio-economic factors like poverty, housing, and unemployment as significant in their lives. In addition, both groups of students raise issues of violence as a barrier to learning. However, family problems and drug use—concerns that have attracted substantial public attention—are less frequently cited by the Aboriginal students in our survey as central problems.

Finally, it is worth noting that a considerable percentage of high school students (33 per cent) say that nothing stands in their way of learning, compared to a much smaller proportion of elementary students (19 per cent). About 12 per cent of high school students, however, rate all teachers as a barrier to learning; elementary students, on the other hand, did not volunteer this information.

The talking circles revealed some insights regarding barriers to education beyond those revealed in the interviews. A strong sense of individual self-determination was a consistent theme in the circles. The students unanimously agreed that blaming outside forces—including historical forces, family members, and government—is not a constructive activity for them and that blaming stands in the way of understanding oneself. They consider collective blaming as a form of 'misguidance'. In addition, the students revealed that taking control of one's language was not only about cultural empowerment but also about personal enrichment. In this regard, they stressed the importance of teaching by Elders because language can be communicated by someone who has 'walked the talk rather than from books'.

Much as in the interviews, the students in the talking circles reiterated how racism and discrimination fundamentally impede learning. They all claimed that teachers in conventional schools may not intend to discriminate, but that these teachers' stereotypical views of First Nations and Métis students prejudge ability and dedication.

Figures 4.7a and 4.7b illustrate what students like about school in general. For both high school and elementary students, it is clear that learning is the most enjoyable part of school and friends are secondary. Although high school students rate teachers as the third most important part of school, elementary students make no mention of teachers, possibly indicating that teachers overall are taken for granted or have less importance for elementary students than for high school students. We may also be seeing an effect of alternative schools for high school students

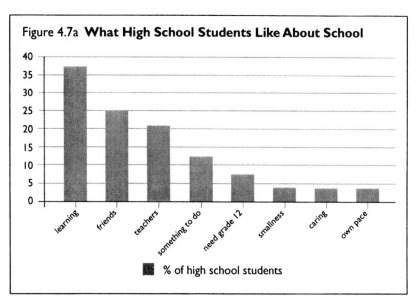

Figure 4.7a **What High School Students Like About School**

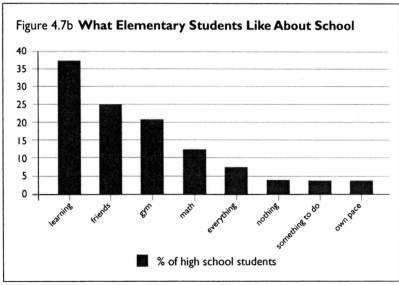

Figure 4.7b **What Elementary Students Like About School**

in that such schools make a concerted effort to engage the students in the decision-making and interactive processes. It is also noteworthy that elementary students mention certain classes or time periods (such as math, gym, or recess) while high school students are more likely to mention the school context, again possibly reflecting the different philosophies and practices in alternative and regular classes, but also possibly reflecting differences in age, maturity, and interest.

When we asked high school students what they like about alternative school relative to conventional school, the responses illustrated the favourable context of alternative programs for high school students. Importantly, all of the students in the alternative schools had previously been in regular schools and in regular programs. Fifty per cent of the students indicated that they like the relaxed atmosphere of alternative schools. Further, they describe the context of the alternative programs by indicating their appreciation of nicer teachers, a more caring atmosphere, and better race relations and cultural learning. When asked specifically about the teachers (Figure 4.8), at least 45 per cent of students answered that they found teachers easy to talk to. Another 30 per cent indicated that sometimes certain teachers were easy to talk to. Only 18 per cent indicated that they did not find it easy in some respect to talk to teachers.

The talking circles revealed that the alternative programs based on cultural teachings provided an important context for educational success. The discussions focused on how the 'warm atmosphere' of the alternative high school programs generated an enthusiasm for learning about culture, an enthusiasm for the pride of accomplishment and what this means for the students themselves as role models for brothers, sisters, and for the next generation, and an enthusiasm for reading in general. The students equated accomplishment in school as a tribute to Elders and the importance of showing 'respect for Elders and others who fought for the right to an education for us'. The students also perceived very clearly that the

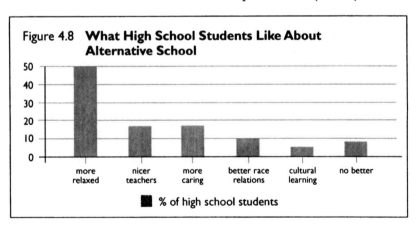

Figure 4.8   **What High School Students Like About Alternative School**

■ % of high school students

route to their success is based on survival in a predominantly white world 'because living in a white culture, you need to learn the white way to keep going to be able to survive.'

The individual interviews revealed some powerful and informative anecdotes about alternative and conventional school systems. The issue of respect is central to the comments:

> What I liked was they gave us a lot of respect, they didn't treat us like a hut full of children, like in some schools I've noticed. They let us be our-selves . . . we were allowed to wear caps and everything in school. It's like, I really liked it.

Another student described the experience of mainstream school and what it meant to him: 'Teachers are nicer here [alternative school]. At the mainstream they are strict and mean . . . hollering and grabbing.' This general experience with teachers led to this student dropping out of school in grade 7 for one year, for which the singular reason given was 'the teacher being too mean'.

Several high school students reiterated their unequivocal appreciation for alternative programs:

> I like the teachers and how nice they are. It's not just do your work, they take the time to help you. If the environment were more friendly in mainstream schools—more down to earth, more relaxed—it would be easier to learn.

> It's [mainstream school] very large and impersonal. A lot of groups really stick together and like maybe they are only friends with people they know . . . like [alternative school] because it's small, caring, and I think, I'm friends with most all of the teachers and everybody, the close-ness I guess, the friendship, that's what really keeps a lot of people here and coming back. And plus, the teachers are great, they don't really make you feel like the whole teacher and student, you know, almost buddies but not so.

> What I like about [alternative school] is the size, it's small and they have a lot of attention they can pay to students. I mean, in mainstream school you are a number, you are on an assembly line basically. Here they have like caring, touch, sensitivity.

In general, these remarks illustrate the relatively high satisfaction that high school students have with their alternative programs. They did have a good deal to say about how to change the conventional school system (Figures 4.9, 4.10a, and 4.10b).

Clearly, the most frequently cited change to schools among the students was the need to incorporate more cultural programming. Second, the students indicated a preference for individual programming. Consistent with previous findings presented in this chapter, students identified important socio-economic issues, specifically racism and poverty, that they felt warranted attention by schools. Only 10 per cent of students indicated that nothing in school should be changed.

When we contrast high school students' views with those of elemen-

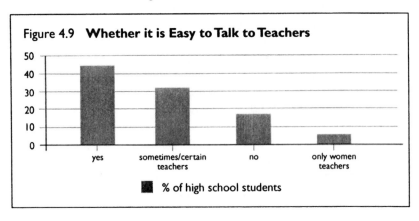

Figure 4.9   **Whether it is Easy to Talk to Teachers**

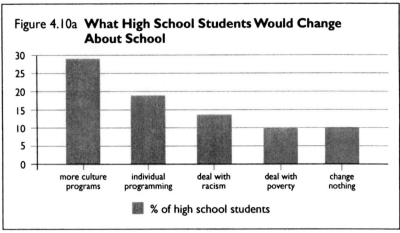

Figure 4.10a   **What High School Students Would Change About School**

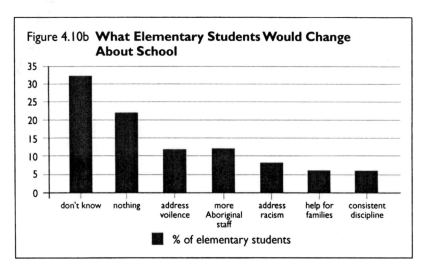

Figure 4.10b **What Elementary Students Would Change About School**

■ % of elementary students

tary school students, it is evident that notwithstanding the large 'don't know' and 'nothing' categories, younger students mention violence, racism, and economic help for families as issues that need to be addressed by schools. They also mention the need for more Aboriginal staff and the need for consistent discipline.

To develop the elementary student school context further, we asked what the students found difficult in school (Figure 4.11).

Almost 30 per cent of the students indicated that they would change nothing about school. With respect to the school curriculum, however,

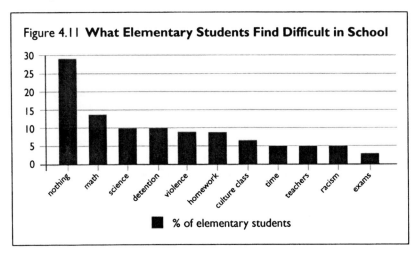

Figure 4.11 **What Elementary Students Find Difficult in School**

■ % of elementary students

students indicated difficulty with math and science and culture class. Again, racism and violence are mentioned as troublesome for some elementary students. These young students also expressed difficulty with homework, exams, teachers, and time management. Overall, then, the difficulties elementary students had in school range from particular subjects to socio-cultural issues like racism and violence.

Within the high school talking circles, the students expressed awareness of the importance of Aboriginal self-determination in education at both the governance and personal levels:

> a long time ago we did not have what we have now so therefore we are now respected for what we are doing. It is up to Aboriginal people to educate ourselves to get what we want and to be who we are. What is taught in the present school system is one-sided to an extent—i.e., in the 1980s, five Aboriginal people were at school based on English and French. So, Aboriginal people refused to learn French because it discriminated against Aboriginal people. It is up to Aboriginal people to force changes to be made.

In addition, the students reiterated the felt need for teachers of Aboriginal ancestry and experience. Further, they expressed the sentiment (and this was a theme that ran through many of the discussions) that students should have greater input into their education with respect to where to go to school, what to take, and the speed at which they are required to complete school. The reality is that for most students in conventional schools there is relatively little latitude regarding where they can go to school, what courses they can take, and the time needed to complete school. The students also suggested that regular schools and alternative programs should allow age flexibility to encourage older students to attend. Their general perception was that schools that had a mix of adult and adolescent students were more comfortable, more democratic, and safer.

The following remarks of a female high school student illustrate another dimension of education that is often unexpressed, possibly because it is considered less of an education issue than one of social welfare. However, the immediacy of the issue to education is expressed in her desire for:

> classes to teach young people what abusive relationships are, how, who you can turn to, how you can get out of it because a lot of times a lot of

people in them or who have gone through them say, 'Well we got this together or he got me this' and they [abuser] usually give money to get their foot back in the door and it usually works.

Finally, the high school students spoke in the talking circles of the importance of language to their overall education. They suggested that when their traditional language is devalued by the school system, elementary students especially develop a distaste for learning in other languages.

Educational Aspirations

We asked both elementary and high school students about their plans to attend post-secondary educational institutions. Figure 4.12 illustrates the results for both types of students.

It is evident that, for students at both levels, the vast majority wish to go to university. The high school group is most noticeable in that almost 70 per cent of the students (in the alternative programs) aspire to university education. Only around 10 per cent of both groups of students do not want to continue with education. These findings indicate a strong commitment to further education and a fairly common resolution to attend university.

We asked all the students to indicate, as well, the types of careers they wish to pursue. The variation in responses was wide. The focus, however, was on professional occupations that demand substantial training. These

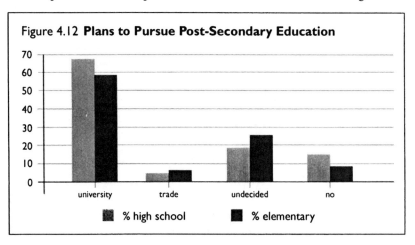

Figure 4.12 **Plans to Pursue Post-Secondary Education**

results follow quite logically from students' high educational aspirations. The careers indicated by high school students included doctor/nurse, lawyer, teacher, business owner, and engineer. Several other occupations included sports and recreation, social work, and police/firefighter. These occupations are all highly relevant to the social and economic needs of the communities and are indicative of a commitment to the local communities. Elementary students indicated similar occupations, with some additional occupations including computers, veterinarian, and mine operator. Overall, both elementary and high school students aspire to occupations that demand a good deal of training and dedication and to occupations that are relevant to their communities. Second, very few students (none in high school and only 10 in elementary) indicated that they did not know what they wanted to be. Obviously, most of the students, despite their ages, do have a focus in that they have given consideration to their careers.

The Relationship between Cultural Education and Educational Outcomes

In this section we relate the prevalence of cultural education programs to the satisfaction that students feel in school, their aspirations, and dropout rates. Figure 4.13 presents the association between whether elementary students like school and whether they receive Aboriginal cultural education in school. The conclusion is drawn by correlating their enjoyment of school with Aboriginal cultural education—two distinct variables.

Here are the results for students who 'like everything about school'. Eleven per cent of the students who indicate that they receive Aboriginal cultural education and 14 per cent who receive a little cultural education indicate that they like everything about school, compared to only 6 per cent of students who receive no cultural education and also 'like everything about school'. Nearly one-third of the students who receive no cultural education 'like nothing about school' compared to those two categories ('yes' and 'a little') that do experience some cultural learning—for which 22 per cent of those who responded 'yes' and 9.5 per cent of those who responded 'a little' among the students also 'like nothing about school'.

As well, the students who like the friendship and social aspects of school are primarily those who receive cultural teaching (33 per cent compared to 12 per cent who do not). Last, it is worth noting that the

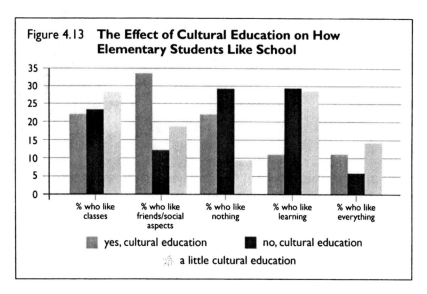

Figure 4.13   **The Effect of Cultural Education on How Elementary Students Like School**

level of cultural education has little impact on whether students like class-es, but cultural education is related to whether students like learning. In this case, it appears that students who receive little or no cultural training in school like the learning aspect of school the most.

One of the more interesting findings is shown in Figure 4.14. Here we find that cultural education is associated with less interest in university and some indecisiveness regarding future education among elementary

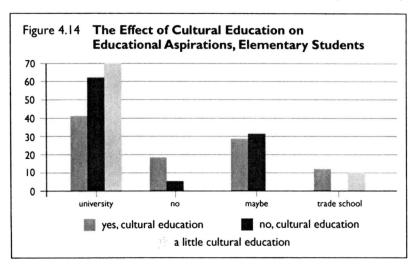

Figure 4.14   **The Effect of Cultural Education on Educational Aspirations, Elementary Students**

students. For example, approximately 40 per cent of those enrolled in cultural education in school desire to go to university compared to 62 per cent not enrolled in cultural education and 70 per cent with little exposure to cultural training. In turn, more students with some or little cultural training indicate they want to go to technical school compared to those with no cultural education. In part, the explanation for this apparent anomaly is that elementary students may not have had the chance or may not have the inclination to think about educational aspirations as much as their high school counterparts. However, it may be that cultural programs, by virtue of their less strictly academic orientation, tend not to focus student aspirations on transition patterns among conventional institutions.

For high school, the results indicate a different pattern of association (Figure 4.15). Here, cultural education has a positive influence on aspirations for higher education. More than four out of five of those students in cultural education programs (either some or a little) in high school want to go to university, compared to half not taking such programs. Although the number of high school students here is small, there may be some indication that the satisfaction students feel with cultural education programs contributes to a desire for higher learning. That may suggest that elementary students who receive some balance of cultural and more traditional academic orientations will develop an interest in post-secondary education over time.

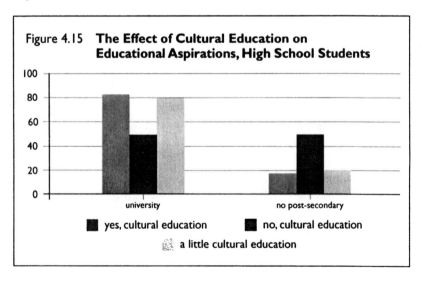

Figure 4.15   The Effect of Cultural Education on Educational Aspirations, High School Students

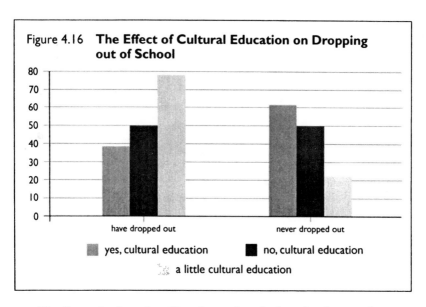

Figure 4.16 **The Effect of Cultural Education on Dropping out of School**

Finally, we look at the effect that cultural education has on dropout rates for the high school students in our sample (Figure 4.16). The results illustrate that cultural education is indeed associated with the likelihood that students will stay in school. Just under 40 per cent of students with cultural education have dropped out of school at least once, compared to 50 per cent of those with no cultural training and 78 per cent of those with little. It is difficult to establish definitely the causal connection between the two variables, but it is defensible that cultural training has a positive influence on students staying in school.

The talking circles revealed some interesting corroborative findings with respect to cultural education. The students unanimously agreed that the teachings of Elders are as important to their lives and their success as the teaching in the formal curriculum. The importance of the teaching and guidance of Elders was endorsed by the talking circle that suggested that Elders' guidance accomplishes two fundamentally important things: because it is based on lifelong learning, it promotes a belief system that learning is a continual process; and, because Elders guide and allow the student to find his/her own values, they encourage one to 'search for knowledge rather than to just accept it'. Their explanation is that Elders' teaching is based on the premise that knowledge comes from within rather than from the outside. They indicate that this passion for learning that is instilled by Elder instruction has a positive effect on their will to seek further education.

When asked the specific things that Elders could bring to the formal school system, the students produced the following litany of skills:

- communication
- listening
- history
- patience
- basic understanding
- acceptance of oneself
- higher self-esteem
- thankfulness
- awareness
- heritage
- respect
- self-discipline
- brotherhood
- friendships
- pride
- self-discovery
- obedience
- faith

The contributions that Elders can make as role models and cultural teachers are similar to what has been reported about the most successful, or exemplary, schools regardless of the racial characteristics of the student body (see, e.g., Gaskell, 1995: 85). In addition, students discussed the principle of 'cleanliness' that informed the teachings of Elders. It is significant that the concept of spiritual and cultural cleanliness is tied to what conventional society might define as cognitive cleanliness, whereby respect for culture and self are the infrastructures of learning. One high school student captured this sentiment as follows:

> One must have clean thoughts, souls, and follow the cultural path. They must keep mother earth clean to show respect. Cleanliness is needed 100 per cent. Aboriginal people have been dirty for so many years by not going to sweats, etc. They are losing out on their culture. Elders have gone so far as to take medicine away, because it was viewed as dirty or seen as using medicines in a negative way versus positive. When you are dirty you can't heal.

Additional Important Issues

Two items appear consistently in the interview and talking circle discussions with high school students: the issue of time and its impact on school success, and pregnancy and child care. On the first issue, over half the students talked about the issue of lateness and how it influenced their time in school. One unsuccessful student related this rather typical experience:

> Interviewer: What was it that you didn't like about there?
> Student: Teachers.
> I: What about the teachers didn't you like?
> S: Because I always got kicked out.
> I: What would they kick you out for?
> S: Talking to people, my homework being late, late for school. I have a problem with being late for school.

Another student's lament illustrates how teacher-student relationships are coloured by time constraints:

> I didn't get along with quite a few of the teachers here. I'm late a lot, that's one of my main problems but I always pass in all my classes. But, I still got held back.

A student with similar concerns suggested that:

> I would change the times in school. I have trouble getting up. I've been getting up lately but before that's why I was held back because I was late. They are thinking of doing that around here, like starting at 11:00 and ending at 6:30.

The issue of lateness is also discussed by some students in the context of cultural bias:

> They want us to go to school but then they kick us out. Last year I was thrown out of school every second time I was late. After a while I just said I didn't want to go to school anymore and I never went. I actually wouldn't kick students out of school for being late but for causing trouble like fighting. Because nowadays you see mostly Aboriginal students

getting kicked out of school and it makes us look like we don't want to learn when that's not true because I've always loved to learn.

Lateness and time constraints are linked to the second problem we discuss in this section, that of child care.

I: What is it that you find difficult or hard about school?
S: Trying to get here because I'm a parent, a single parent, and sometimes my son gets sick and I have to miss, and it's the work, like it's two-hour-long classes that I have to miss, and I fall behind and I can never get back, I just keep falling behind.

Another student discussed how the particular daycare program in the alternative school in which she was registered improved the quality of her education and her life:

I remember when my son was really young, it was really hard to find daycare facilities but now I don't think is as bad. With the centre in the school it really helped me find good babysitters, like good quality babysitters.

The same student discussed why school-based daycare centres are substantially better than community-based centres:

a lot of these daycare homes, they want you to pick up your child right after school and that's kinda hard to make the transition. First, you're at school and have all this work to do, and then pick up your kid, take the bus, the bus is horrible but that's a whole other story.

This last experience accentuates the need of young student/parents for a school that not only provides the daycare facility but also opportunities to develop parenting skills, and that encourages parenting as something that can enhance learning and happiness. One older student revealed in the talking circles how she is a mother of a five-year-old and previously had a substance abuse problem. Before coming to the alternative school, she had found parenting a burden and had never, as a result, 'played with her child'—she had never actually taken her child to a playground. After spending time in the alternative program, she had learned how to enjoy time with her child and now found that to be the most rewarding part of her life. She indicated that, as a result, her substance abuse problem was under control and the new-found happiness with her child had dramatically increased her happiness and success in school.

SUMMARY

The research findings presented in this chapter demonstrate that Aboriginal youth in Saskatchewan schools have very definite views about their schooling experiences and educational plans. In contrast to characteristic perceptions of an uneasy relationship between Aboriginal people and schools, our research findings indicate that First Nations and Métis students in the elementary and alternative high schools chosen for the study have generally positive assessments of their education and have adopted a serious orientation to learning and aspirations for the future. They tend to enjoy learning, particularly in selected subject areas, they frequently have good relationships with their teachers, and they value friendships and cultural aspects of schooling. They also express relatively ambitious educational and career aspirations that suggest a long-term commitment to education.

The Aboriginal students we surveyed demonstrate, as well, a high degree of awareness of social, economic, and historical factors that influence their schooling. They see their prospects for educational success affected by problems within and outside of schools. In school, while most students report having had access to Aboriginal cultural programming and Aboriginal teachers, such exposure is often limited in nature, restricted to specific subject areas or time periods apart from mainstream programming. Students also express some concerns about intolerant teachers, inconsistent disciplinary standards, inflexible time arrangements, and problems with certain subjects (science and math are most frequently cited, but the latter is identified by other students as an area that they like) that stand as barriers to their learning prospects. More generally, they identify issues like racism, prejudice, poverty, violence, and unemployment as factors that may intervene into their lives in such a way as to affect their prospects for educational success. They value teachers and programming that are sensitive to their cultures. In each of these regards, their positive commitment to and assessment of schooling are enhanced when respect and cultural understanding are integrated into their educational environments. Their motivation to succeed is driven to a large extent by a combination of respect for their Elders and individual strength and development.

DISCUSSION

Drawing on data from interviews and talking circles conducted with First Nations and Métis students in the subject schools, their expressions that we present here highlight four related sets of factors.

1. *Culture in the educational context.* The Aboriginal students we interviewed both in elementary and high schools place considerable importance on their cultural heritage. Aboriginal languages are spoken in the homes of nearly all of these students, and all but 30 per cent of the elementary students and 40 per cent of the high school students could speak at least some Aboriginal language. In their schools, a substantial proportion of the students surveyed are exposed to Cree language classes, Native studies classes, Aboriginal history, and spirituality, but students expressed a desire for even greater teaching of Aboriginal languages and ceremonies than they currently receive.

2. *Student perceptions of school experience.* The students interviewed are highly positive about their school experiences, but they encounter a variety of problems and barriers to their learning. Racism and discrimination are their most prevalent concerns, particularly among Aboriginal students in high school. Students also see connections between such socio-economic factors as unemployment, housing, poverty, hunger, and violence, and their learning prospects. At the same time, students enjoy learning and express a high degree of motivation to succeed. They see the need to link their own schooling success with appreciation for the knowledge and experience of their Elders. Students in the alternative school setting report the highest degree of compatibility towards fulfillment of the linkages between their cultural heritage and educational aspirations. Students in provincial schools want schools to incorporate more cultural programming, a greater degree of programming to meet individual needs, and sensitivity to racism, poverty, and other socio-economic issues.

3. *Educational aspirations.* Students express a strong commitment to further education, with only about 10 per cent indicating that they do not wish to continue their schooling beyond high school. Most students seek careers that require post-secondary education, in professions like medicine, nursing, law, teaching, and engineering. Business ownership and community-related occupations involving sports and recreation and community service are also widely cited as desirable careers. Nearly all students are focused insofar as they have a definite conception of their career aspirations.

4. *The effect of cultural education on educational outcomes.* Aboriginal students who are exposed to cultural programming are the most likely to like schooling, while those with no cultural programming are least likely to enjoy schooling. Elementary school students who receive cultural training in schools are less likely to aspire to university education, but in high school there is a strong desire by students who have cultural education programs to attend university. Students who receive cultural programming are less likely to drop out of school than those who do not. Aboriginal students place a high value on the role that Elders play in their lives, both directly through their involvement in schools and indirectly through their lives and examples.

Among high school students surveyed, two additional items are important—the need for schools to recognize how the organization of time affects learning prospects and the need to recognize the concerns specific to demands and skills associated with parenting and child care.

CONCLUSIONS

There are several encouraging signs in the overall positive assessments that Aboriginal students make of their schooling experiences. There is also a need to integrate further cultural programming and personnel into the schools, while schools must recognize that Aboriginal culture encompasses particular socio-economic and personal concerns as well as traditional heritage, and many Aboriginal Canadians are highly disadvantaged people relative to mainstream Canada. Students demonstrate a desire for educational achievement and career aspirations consistent with success by conventional standards, but they also seek grounding in their cultural traditions and practices so that they can operate in two integrated worlds.

The Importance of the Student Voice in Research on Aboriginal Education

We have emphasized that education has been for several decades one of the most pressing issues for Canada's Aboriginal people. Since the National Indian Brotherhood's declaration in 1972 that 'Indian control of Indian education' was to be the crucial factor in the struggle by Aboriginal people to regain their identity and establish an equitable footing in Canadian society, much has changed even as many things have remained the same. First Nations have established control over innovative educational programs and institutions, new measures have been introduced to increase educational participation and attainment by Aboriginal people, and Aboriginal content has been integrated into or even become a central part of curricula and programs in many education systems.

Nonetheless, further progress is needed to address serious problems on several fronts. Educational attainment among Aboriginal people remains well below comparable levels for the general population while school dropout rates are much higher, and uneasy relations are frequently cited between Aboriginal communities and the schools that serve them. These problems are all the more serious in a public context in which education is increasingly looked to as a hallmark of social and economic success. We have already emphasized, reinforcing the assessment of the Royal Commission on Aboriginal Peoples (1996b: 5), that Aboriginal people, in general, continue to experience serious economic marginalization and social disintegration along several dimensions, including high unemployment, low labour force participation, economic dependency, poor health, and high rates of incarceration.

While these concerns have serious implications for Aboriginal people and the general population alike, they are most deeply felt by Aboriginal children and youth for whom progressive advances in educational, occupational, and social opportunities are intertwined with continuing barriers to their success. Paradoxically, despite the mounting body of research on Aboriginal issues, much of which has finally begun to acknowledge repeated demands for representation and control by Aboriginal people themselves, little research has incorporated the voices of First Nations and Métis children and youth. The present study is a response to this concern by way of examining how young Aboriginal people view their schooling experiences in relation to other aspects of their lives.

This chapter has examined several dimensions of Aboriginal students' experiences in Saskatchewan schools, with particular emphasis on how the students perceive schooling and other factors that influence their chances for educational success. The three main research questions have been answered as follows.

1. *What factors do First Nations and Métis students identify as the strengths and limitations of their schooling?* The First Nations and Métis students surveyed in our research highlight several strengths and limitations in their schooling experiences. Most notably, the students offer, overall, a positive assessment of their schools both in general and with respect to more specific dimensions of their education. There are encour-

aging signs insofar as high proportions of students indicate that they have had exposure to Aboriginal teachers and, to a lesser extent, to programs and cultural activities related to their heritage. It is apparent, however, that Aboriginal personnel and curricula are not as centrally integrated into provincial schools and school programming as student demand would warrant. Elementary and high school students find that their teachers, with a few exceptions, facilitate their learning and are accessible and approachable. The students also convey a strong orientation to learning and a desire to succeed in conventional terms. The students' responses to specific questions and their discussions in talking circles indicate their concurrence with the dominant public sentiment that places a high value on education and its importance for future life opportunities. They are motivated by a desire to extend their education into post-secondary studies and seek professional and vocational careers that require advanced educational credentials. These motivations are reinforced with respect for Elders and a drive to demonstrate personal empowerment.

Like other students, Aboriginal students indicate that they have some difficulty with regular features of school such as particular subjects, school rules, homework, discipline, exams, and interactions with selected teachers, although none of these is posed as a serious limitation to learning. The barriers and limitations that emerge in a more pronounced way tend to be related to specific dimensions of First Nations and Métis experience. Racism, prejudice, and discrimination appear frequently as important considerations in student accounts of their relations with teachers, other students, and people outside of school. Whether these factors constitute part of students' individual encounters or are transmitted to them through the lives and stories of those close to them, they correspond to the sense of vulnerability and discomfort that Aboriginal people feel with mainstream educational institutions, as conveyed in much of the literature cited in previous chapters. By contrast, those students who report that their schools are more sensitive to Aboriginal students and their cultures, especially in the alternative school setting surveyed in our research, indicate greater degrees of comfort and engagement in the schooling process.

2. *How relevant is schooling, according to the perceptions of First Nations and Métis students, to their out-of-school experiences and aspirations?* The students we surveyed report that their schooling exhibits some sensitivity to Aboriginal content, and they view education as important to their futures. As indicated above, they value education and have little

inclination to modify many of the central features of current education systems. These findings seem to contradict the theme of cultural dislocation that is conveyed in much of the literature on Aboriginal people's historical relationships with the education system, but they are consistent with the search by First Nations and Métis communities for meaningful participation and decision-making roles in education. In these respects, the students convey a desire to have access to quality education, meet educational standards, and pursue futures that require high levels of educational attainment, but they report the greatest satisfaction and confidence when their schooling is supported by respect for their cultural heritage and circumstances.

Culture must be understood here as a complex and changing phenomenon. In a limited sense, cultural teaching is reported in various forms through instruction in Native languages, Native studies courses, traditional stories, spirituality, and involvement by Elders and Aboriginal teachers in schooling. Aboriginal students value the inclusion of these factors in the school system, but they feel that even greater steps must be taken to accommodate fully their cultural needs. More broadly, culture also refers to the ongoing social and economic conditions that characterize students' lives, including the legacy of past traditions and more recent experiences. The relevance of schooling in this regard depends on its ability to incorporate sensitivity to life experience in a holistic manner.

3. *What is the relationship between these student perceptions and various social factors in and out of school?* Among the issues that inform their realities, as related by many students who participated in our research, are racism, discrimination, poverty, violence and abuse, housing problems, parenting and domestic relations, and unemployment. While these problems are not universally experienced, or shared to the same extent, student sensitivity to their importance indicates a need for educators and school officials to remain vigilant to the context within which schools operate and to the needs, beyond standard curricular concerns, that students bring with them into the classroom. Aboriginal students want to do well, and have high aspirations that require educational success, but they face continual reminders that their participation in schools may often be somewhat fragile as they are confronted with situations at home, in their communities, and at school that may lead to lowered performance and expectations, withdrawal, or failure. It is noteworthy, for instance, that few of the students aspire to occupations as general labourers or employees, or to futures out of school that are even more restricted, despite sta-

tistical projections and trends that suggest a much harsher reality for large segments of the Aboriginal population.

Overall, our research suggests that educational attainment and success among Aboriginal students can be enhanced when schools embrace programs, practices, and personnel that are informed by a combination of conventional and Aboriginal-specific sensitivities. Students desire achievement and seek futures determined by conventional standards, but they also seek grounding in their cultural traditions and practices in such a way that they can operate successfully in two, hopefully integrated, worlds.

QUESTIONS FOR CRITICAL THOUGHT

1. Discuss the importance of including children and youth in research on education. To what extent can they be considered reliable sources of data for such research?
2. Discuss the importance of language and culture, as viewed by Aboriginal students, to the schooling experience.
3. Which educational factors do Aboriginal students consider to be limitations to their schooling, and which ones do they find to be enabling and enhancing? Discuss the importance of these observations for educational policy and planning.
4. Critically compare and contrast Aboriginal students' accounts of conventional schooling and alternative schools. What implications do these observations have for designing effective educational programs for Aboriginal students and other learners?
5. Given what you have heard from students in this chapter, is there a possibility that the existing conventional education system could adapt to the needs of Aboriginal students? Or, is a new paradigm needed for education? Please explain your position.

RECOMMENDED READING

Alladin, Ibrahim. 1996. *Racism in Canadian Schools*. Toronto: Harcourt Brace and Company.

This book offers a comprehensive view of the historical and contemporary forces that generate both institutional and overt racism in Canadian schools. The author presents a theoretical challenge for understanding discrimination in education and a formula for anti-racist education.

Gatto, John Taylor. 1992. *Dumbing Us Down: The Hidden Curriculum of Compulsory Schooling.* Gabriola Island, BC: New Society Publishers.

This is a compelling study of the problems with compulsory state-sponsored schooling. Gatto's position, based on years of teaching in public school in New York, is that formal education stands in the way of students learning about the world around them and that community-based learning through mentoring and experience provides a fundamentally better preparation for life than formal in-class instruction.

Hern, Matt. 1996. *Deschooling Our Lives.* Gabrioloa Island, BC: New Society Publishers.

This book draws on the thinking of some of the most important historical and contemporary writers in education and education philosophy. Hern considers what parents are doing instead of sending their children to conventional schools and challenges our thinking about the usefulness and effectiveness of conventional education.

Schissel, Bernard. 1997. *Blaming Children: Youth Crime, Moral Panics and the Politics of Hate.* Halifax: Fernwood.

The author documents how the print media in Canada construct images of bad children and youth largely on the basis of their social marginality, and discusses how the media fashion racialized, gendered, and class-based images of youth that conform to the general public's understanding of modern youth as particularly dangerous and disrespectful. The importance of education in understanding 'moral panics' surrounding youth is that the inability of a young person to do well in school, or the individual's perceived cognitive impairment, is often used as part of a damning biography.

CHAPTER 5

DETERMINANTS OF
SUCCESSFUL SCHOOLING

INTRODUCTION

In this chapter, we explore the prospects for Aboriginal people to move beyond the detrimental impact of residential schooling and other previous educational and social experiences. Formal education is widely accepted as a crucial gateway to participation in social, economic, and political spheres of life. Concomitantly, social opportunities tend to diminish for persons who lack educational credentials. We have examined, in previous chapters, several dimensions of these relationships, especially with regard to what is often known as the 'education gap' between Aboriginal people and other Canadians. Our focus lies with factors associated with the facilitation of and barriers to educational success. While the discussion is guided by the nature and organization of formal education systems, particularly in the form of public schooling, we also examine alternative school systems and conceptions of education that extend beyond formal schooling. In order to frame this analysis, we begin the chapter with an overview of labour market circumstances and options for Aboriginal people, since contemporary education is so closely associated with (even though it must not be considered exclusively or even primarily as preparation for) employment and economic opportunities.

Two major themes have dominated the literature on the schooling experiences and probabilities of educational success or failure among Aboriginal children and youth. First, and most prominent, is the proliferation of studies that detail the dimensions of the long-standing gap between Aboriginal students and the general population with respect to educational attainment, school leaving and dropout rates, in-school problems, and associated socio-economic concerns (see, e.g., Frideres, 1998; Satzewich and Wotherspoon, 2000; Royal Commission on Aboriginal Peoples, 1996c). A second, growing body of literature describes a wide range of initiatives, including education and employment equity measures, cultural training, curriculum development and modification, and opportunities for greater involvement by Aboriginal people in diverse educational settings (Assembly of First Nations, 1988; Kirkness and Bowman, 1992; Royal Commission on Aboriginal Peoples, 1996c). This combination of optimism and pessimism about the state of education for Aboriginal people is matched by mixed evidence about how successful these initiatives have been (Hamilton, 1991; Royal Commission on Aboriginal Peoples, 1993, 1996c; Mills Consulting, 1992, 1993).

Determinants of potential educational success or failure operate at several interdependent levels. One encouraging trend in the literature is the shift in focus away from a preoccupation to locate the source of educational problems within the individual students or Aboriginal cultures. Instead, analysis has come to emphasize how social, organizational, and policy arrangements, such as residential schooling, educational finance, and curricula, have affected educational practices and outcomes (see especially Deyhle and Swisher, 1997, for a comprehensive review of the literature, albeit with an American focus). The most important of these considerations are outlined later in the chapter with respect to in-school factors (related to teachers, students, curricula, and programming), alternative conceptions and forms of education, and educational governance and resources. However, this discussion begins and concludes with the reference to the social and economic contexts in which schooling is organized, and the communities that schools are intended to serve, in order to highlight the interdependent relationships between schooling and out-of-school factors that are central to the understanding of educational matters in general.

THE RELATIONSHIP BETWEEN EDUCATION AND ECONOMIC PARTICIPATION

Before we consider some of the main contributions that education systems make to the relative success or failure of Aboriginal children and youth, we pose the question of what prospects exist for those learners beyond schooling. This issue is an important one, since it requires that we take seriously and engage critically the widespread assumption that more education, in itself, is a good thing—it forces us to address, first, what people are missing out on when they do not achieve necessary levels of education and, second, the prospects those people would face if the education gap could be eliminated.

Table 5.1 Aboriginal Ancestry by Highest Level of Education, Ages 15 and Over, 1996

Highest Level of Education	Total Population	Visible Minority	Total Aboriginal Ancestry	Métis	Inuit	North American Indians	On-Reserve*	Off-Reserve*
Less than high school	25.8	23.0	42.2	39.8	43.1	43.1	48.3 (40.0)**	40.2 (60.0)
Secondary	16.3	14.7	10.7	12.7	7.2	10.1	8.1 (28.6)	11.2 (71.4)
Trades certificate or diploma only	4.2	2.3	4.6	4.6	6.6	4.4	5.7 (46.1)	3.7 (53.9)
Some post-secondary	18.4	22.9	20.2	19.0	20.7	20.8	18.8 (32.3)	21.8 (67.7)
Post-secondary certificate or diploma	20.2	15.3	18.2	19.3	20.5	17.6	16.6 (33.5)	18.2 (66.5)
University degree or certificate	15.1	21.9	4.1	4.6	1.9	4.1	2.5 (22.1)	4.9 (77.9)
Total number	19,901,705	2,142,230	416,565	122,500	16,075	281,910	100,460	181,455

*On-reserve and off-reserve totals for North American Indians only.
**All numbers in parentheses represent the particular cell as a percentage of the number found under the North American Indians column and within the same row.
Source: Compiled from Statistics Canada, Catalogue numbers 94F0009XDB96001 and 94F0009XDB96000. The total population differs by 15 between Statistics Canada publications 94F0009XDB96001 and 94F0009XDB96003

Table 5.2 Selected Labour Force and Income Characteristics of Canada's Aboriginal Population, Ages 15 and Over, 1996

	Total Population	Visible Minority	Total Aboriginal Ancestry	Métis	Inuit	North American Indians	On-Reserve*	Off-Reserve*
Labour force participation rate	65.5	63.6	58.3	64.8	60.0	55.6	51.1	58.6
Employed	58.9	54.6	44.3	51.6	47.0	41.2	36.4 (35.4)**	44.4 (64.6)
Unemployed	6.6	9.0	14.0	13.2	13.0	14.4	14.7 (40.9)	14.2 (59.1)
Not in labour force	34.5	36.4	41.7	35.2	40.0	44.4	48.9 (44.1)	41.4 (55.9)
Unemployment rate	10.1	14.2	24.0	20.4	21.7	25.9	28.8	24.2
With employment income	92.4	86.5	90.7	90.9	89.0	90.7	50.6	89.2
Without employment income	7.6	13.5	9.3	9.1	11.0	9.3	49.4	10.8
Average income $ (those employed)	25,196	20,158	15,699	17,639	16,819	14,864	12,252	16,678
Median income $ (those employed)	18,891	14,438	10,998	12,362	11,086	10,500	8,899	11,676
Total population	22,628,925	2,419,140	518,590	144,160	24,130	354,780	142,055***	212,720

* On-reserve and off-reserve totals for North American Indians only.
**All numbers in parentheses represent the particular cell as a percentage of the number found under the North American Indians column and within the same row.
***There is a difference of five cases between the labour force activity total and the income grouping totals.
Source: Compiled from Statistics Canada, Catalogue numbers 94F0009XDB96001 and 94F0009XDB96003. All figures based on a 20 per cent sample of the 1996 census.

It is important to recognize formal education as both a contributing factor to and product of people's social and economic circumstances. Levels of educational attainment and the quality of educational experiences are strongly associated with social background characteristics. In the same way that having more formal education is likely to improve the chances that a person (and other members of his or her household) has to secure employment, better income, good health, and other social benefits, those people who come from households with higher income or education levels to begin with are best situated to secure educational advantage. Guppy and Davies (1998: 119), summarizing both the recent literature and national data on educational attainment in Canada, emphasize that 'social class, as measured by either occupation or education of parents, still matters.' Moreover, they observe that while educational disparities have tended to ease with regard to such factors as gender, race and ethnicity, and disability status, persistent inequalities remain for selected groups, most notably First Nations and people of Portuguese ancestry, which in turn reflect class-based inequalities (ibid., 123). This is not to suggest that Aboriginal educational matters can be reduced only to class or socio-economic factors, but it does point to the need to understand schooling in relation to the contexts within which it takes place as well as to the characteristics and experiences that its participants bring with them.

The data in Tables 5.1 and 5.2 provide a summary of some of the major indicators of educational and economic differentiation between Aboriginal people and other Canadians, as well as within the Aboriginal population. They demonstrate that, as a whole, Aboriginal people fare much worse than the general population in terms of their education and income levels and labour force participation. This disparity holds even when Aboriginal people are compared with other racial minorities (the official definition of visible minority in Canada does not include Aboriginal people). However, there are also substantial differences in these measures within the Aboriginal population. The Inuit and First Nations people living on reserves experience by far the poorest educational and economic circumstances. This, of course, is partly a reflection of geographic isolation because educational and employment opportunities are more likely to be concentrated in metropolitan centres than in remote areas where many reserves and Inuit communities are located. Nonetheless, the data also demonstrate significant variation in living conditions, opportunities, services, and policy needs among diverse sectors of the Aboriginal population.

These figures provide a useful overview, but they do not reveal the factors that give rise to them. More accurate comparisons can be made by examining the impact of variables like age, region, gender, and community structures. Analysis conducted by Bernier (1997: 11), for instance, suggests that age, education, and work-related factors can account for about 60 per cent of the average earnings difference between Aboriginal and non-Aboriginal populations. Other conditions, such as the relatively young age profile of the Aboriginal population and locale (as many reserves and Inuit communities are in rural and remote regions where social infrastructures and economic opportunities are limited), also contribute to observed differences among populations (ibid., 10–11; Department of Indian and Northern Affairs, 1997: 20 ff.). Similarly, the prevalence among segments of the Aboriginal population of such factors as higher than average rates of poverty, accident, disease, injury, incarceration, and lone-parent family structures, and limited access to housing, child care, and other vital services, all reflect and contribute to reduced prospects for education, employment, and income.

Another way to examine comparisons with groups is to examine occupational and labour market characteristics. As has been observed, there is a general tendency for employment prospects and income to increase with educational qualifications or credentials. Young Aboriginal adults who had not completed high school at the time of the 1996 census had an unemployment rate of 40 per cent, over four times the rate of 9 per cent for those with a university degree (Tait, 1999: 6). Posed in another way, nearly half of working-age Aboriginal people had not completed high school; for those who were employed, just below one-third had not completed high school. At the other extreme, 36.3 per cent of those who were employed, compared with 25.6 per cent of all Aboriginal people of working age, had post-secondary certificates or degrees (Government of Canada, 1999: 3).

Census data reveal that, for Aboriginal people who worked on a full-time, full-year basis, average earnings were $24,815 for those with less than grade 9, $28,157 for those who had graduated from high school, and $42,220 for those with a university degree (Statistics Canada, 1998c: 12). These tendencies hold true for people from all social categories, but the return from education is distributed unequally. Attaining higher educational credentials also makes a difference to earnings. Having a high school certificate, compared to having less than grade 9, increased average earnings by 25 per cent for Aboriginal people and by 18 per cent for the general population, while completion of a university degree, relative to high school completion, increased earnings by a further 82 per cent overall for Aboriginal people and 89 per cent for the population as a whole (calculated from ibid., 5, 12). Nonetheless, the average earnings in 1995 for Aboriginal people who had a university degree and who worked on a full-time, full-year basis were just under $200 more than the average earnings of all workers in Canada with a university degree, even though the latter is reduced by the inclusion of persons who worked on a part-time and seasonal basis. Analysis of census data produced for the Canadian Race Relations Foundation demonstrates that Aboriginal people and other visible minorities were more likely than other Canadians to be unemployed or underemployed relative to their levels of education (Canadian Council on Social Development, 2000: 19–20). The same report summarizes the occupational circumstances of racialized and non-racialized groups. Aboriginal people increasingly are finding employment across a wide range of fields, with growing representation in such areas as managerial and professional work and skilled labour, which normally require substantial levels of formal training or educational credentials. However, the highest concentrations of Aboriginal employees are found in clerical and service occupations, unskilled trades, and other areas that tend to be characterized by low wages and poor working conditions. Aboriginal people are highly underrepresented in semi-professional and semi-skilled trades areas (Government of Canada, 1999: 3). Even among those in managerial and professional positions, or in other jobs that involve better wages, benefits, and working conditions, Aboriginal people tend to be concentrated in lower or mid-level positions, in temporary or seasonal work, or in sectors that lack prospects for long-term career security and advancement (Canadian Council on Social Development, 2000: 20, 25).

The Royal Commission on Aboriginal Peoples (1996d: 806 ff.) suggests that distinct economies or labour market conditions correspond roughly to the disparate circumstances experienced by Aboriginal people in urban centres, on First Nations reserves and in Métis communities, and in the Far North. Each of these sectors contains unique configurations of resources, services, demographic profiles, employment opportunities, and requirements for labour force qualifications, as well as divergent profiles of skills, training, and educational credentials. In 1996, for example, about 4 per cent of Aboriginal people in their twenties who lived in cities of 100,000 people or more, compared to just over 1 per cent of those who lived on rural reserves, had university degrees. This model is useful for demonstrating the multi-faceted nature of economic and social conditions, even though it does oversimplify the much more complex social and economic relationships that prevail within Aboriginal populations, their interactions with others, and the social and economic structures that underlie these relations.

In a context in which the virtues of schooling are widely promoted, we must be careful not to overlook the fact that many jobs and industries do not require a direct connection with university degrees or other forms of formal education that tend to carry the most prestige. Aboriginal people are overrepresented in employment in resource industries like fishing, trapping, forestry and logging, and mining (Government of Canada, 1999: 3), many of which do not require substantial training and are located in or near the rural regions or traditional lands in which employees live. Many growing economic sectors or occupations in which there remain high demands for new workers are seeking entrants with minimal skills (such as sales or services), or those who hold specific forms of certification or training (such as trucking or construction trades) that do not require extensive investments of time in formal educational settings (Human Resources Development Canada, 2000). Similarly, as we will discuss later in the chapter, employers fail to recognize substantial bodies of knowledge, skills, and other capacities within many Aboriginal communities and segments of the population because they do not have formal credentials attached to them. Nonetheless, the growing premium that is placed on educational qualifications and experiences is a result of the growing sense of importance that education contributes to general social capabilities, as well as to the knowledge and skills that have been attained in their own rights. Educational credentials often are used by employers and institutions as a screening mechanism for entry into other educational or trades-training programs, or in making selections from large numbers of job applicants even in circumstances where those credentials appear to have no direct relevance or are not established or explicit requirements. More generally, employers and representatives of other agencies typically regard general educational achievement as a mark of social capability and, conversely, hold less regard for persons who have limited educational attainment.

There are some promising signs in that Aboriginal people, generally, are gaining more formal education and studying in a broader range of fields than previously. Census data reveal that, between 1991 and 1996, the proportions of Aboriginal people who had not completed high school declined for each age cohort 20 years and over—from 57 to 53 per cent for those aged 20 to 24, from 52 to 44 per cent for those aged 25 to 34, and from 61 to 50 per cent for those in the 35–64 age cohort—while proportions who had completed college, trades, and university programs increased for each of these cohorts (Canadian Council on Social Development, 2000: 16). Even more encouraging, higher than average proportions of Aboriginal people are returning to school or entering post-secondary programs later in life. During the same 1991–6 period, Aboriginal people who had some post-secondary education remained heavily concentrated in business, commerce, and engineering fields (which together accounted for about half of the Aboriginal students aged 25–44 in post-secondary studies in 1996), with building technology trades such as construction, plumbing, and welding attracting most of this enrolment. Increasing proportions of Aboriginal students are enrolling in social sciences, agriculture, and biological science, while more traditional areas such as education, nursing and health care, fine arts, and humanities reveal relatively stable enrolment trends (ibid., 18; Tait, 1999: 9).

Trends indicating that Aboriginal people are extending their schooling and studying in a broader range of fields provide some indication that educational and occupational prospects among Aboriginal people are likely to improve and diversify. At the same time, it is clear that there is considerable under-utilization of the educational capacity of Aboriginal people, and significant limitations of access to and realization of educational opportunities remain. Despite improvements, these barriers operate at virtually all educational levels, and they have a compounding impact on future opportunities for personal and social advancement. Each step that serves as a filter to remove Aboriginal learners from education and training systems results in reduced prospects that educational, occupational, and social positions in higher levels can be filled (Working Margins Consulting Group, 1992: 50). While it is possible to track many individual success stories through the advancement of educational opportunities, considerable efforts will be required to bridge the education gap for large segments of the population. There is little evidence that such effort is being expended; therefore, there is unlikely to be substantial movement, at least in the near future, away from educational pathways that reproduce existing occupational patterns and inequalities.

These observations, consistent with our discussion in the previous chapters, indicate that we must not reduce policy matters related to education, training, and employment prospects to the level of particular individuals. Individual motivation and initiative are crucial components of educational success that are fostered and enabled in appropriate family, community, and social contexts, but motivation and initiative are influenced also by broader dynamics of labour markets, social opportunities, and underlying forms of inequality that prevail more generally. The next sections of this chapter explore crucial dimensions of schooling, informed by sensitivity to its place within these broader contexts that contribute to increasing prospects for success among Aboriginal students.

IN-SCHOOL FACTORS AS DETERMINANTS OF EDUCATIONAL SUCCESS

The likelihood of educational success for Aboriginal students is affected by several aspects of the schooling process. As with any students, the ways in which children of Aboriginal ancestry experience their relations with teachers, peers, school rules and procedures, and subjects and curricula have a significant impact on their schooling careers and later lives. Aboriginal children and youth often face additional pressures to the extent that they are confronted with racism, language barriers, cultural misunderstandings, and school climates that they are unfamiliar with or that may even be hostile to them. Some of the most important processes, identified through research findings relevant to these issues, are summarized in the next two sections, which address, respectively, teacher-student relations and curriculum issues.

Teachers, Pedagogies, and Aboriginal Students

Educational researchers and members of Aboriginal communities have stressed repeatedly both the need for and the educational benefits of having teachers who understand Aboriginal cultures and are sensitive to the specific needs of Indian and Métis learners. Stairs (1995: 146–7) describes the role of teachers as 'cultural brokers' who mediate between indigenous and non-indigenous worlds through their selection and presentation of ideas, values, knowledge, and interpersonal relationships. It must be stressed that the literature is not conclusive on the issue of whether Aboriginal teachers, in themselves, contribute to greater educational success among Aboriginal students. Nonetheless, the presence of teachers who share a common heritage with the students they teach fosters a sense of acceptance and may facilitate stronger communication among education system personnel, students, and parents.

Data on the representation and distribution of teachers of Aboriginal ancestry in Canadian schools are sketchy at best. The Royal Commission on Aboriginal Peoples (1996c: 491) estimates that the Aboriginal teaching force would have to triple in size from current levels to approach parity with the numbers of non-Aboriginal teachers who work with Aboriginal students. In Saskatchewan, where school divisions in which at least 5 per cent of students are of Aboriginal ancestry are encouraged to develop and report annually on approved education equity plans, Aboriginal teachers increased from 4.2 to 5.5 per cent of the teaching force overall in the designated districts, while comparable proportions of Aboriginal students increased from 16.1 to 20.4 per cent between 1989 and 1999 (calculated from Saskatchewan Human Rights Commission, 1999).

Despite selected improvements in the hiring and retention of Aboriginal teachers in some schools and districts, equity objectives are still far from being achieved. Many post-secondary institutions have introduced teacher education programs oriented to training teachers who work in a variety of Aboriginal community contexts, thereby contributing to an increased supply of and more supportive environment for Aboriginal teachers. However, despite their equivalency with general teacher training programs, such programs are often stigmatized and devalued, regarded as inferior or lacking standards. Teachers of Aboriginal ancestry often identify similar difficulties in the way they are treated or regarded within their teaching environments. They commonly report credibility problems as well as other concerns, such as stereotyping and racism, lack of support from other teachers and administrators, and segregation into teaching roles as Aboriginal or Native studies specialists even when they do not seek or feel qualified for those responsibilities (Melnechenko and Horseman, 1998: 125; St Denis et al., 75–6). Many Aboriginal teachers, even when they are gratified that they can serve as role models for students, seek validation through their identity as teachers more than as indigenous people. Consistent with orientations adopted by teachers from other minority backgrounds, teachers of Aboriginal ancestry may attempt to deny their heritage and adopt 'raceless' identities, even if these are not accepted by non-Aboriginal colleagues, in order to meet perceived expectations about what a 'good teacher' is (Hesch, 1995: 125).

Ironically, the most critical factors in teaching success tend to be associated less with what any teacher's racial or social background is than with the degree to which teachers are sensitive to student backgrounds and cultural orientations, including possible differences in learning styles (Campbell, 1991: 109–10). Even at the university level, Aboriginal students respond most favourably to instructors whose pedagogical approach is based on honest, caring interpersonal relationships rather than simply a professional orientation to strong instruction and accessibility (Wilson, 1994: 311–12). Teachers, in these regards, must be able to adopt an integrated rather than a piecemeal approach to Aboriginal issues. To accomplish this, they must have a comprehensive knowledge of the meaning and nature of cultural practices among various First Nations traditions (Archibald, 1995: 352–3). Partly for these reasons, there are increasing demands for schools to hire more Aboriginal teachers and involve Elders in educational programming. Their presence is important both symbolically, as a sign of openness and acceptance by the school system towards Indian and Métis communities, and in practical terms for the particular experiences and learning that those teachers and Elders may share with students, staff, and administrators (National Indian Brotherhood/Assembly of First Nations, 1988: 154).

In addition, it is important to recognize that students and their parents do not only desire Aboriginal content and traditional cultural elements. They also place strong value on programming and staff that are oriented to understand and respond to the concerns and issues that students may bring with them into the classroom from outside school. Cultural sensitivity in these regards is not isolated to issues related to heritage, but must encompass a deeper regard for the social relations and environmental realities that characterize student life.

Discussions and initiatives to transform education to better serve the needs of Aboriginal learners, as for any other group, must also be informed by sensitivity to the work roles and capabilities of teachers. Students, parents, community members, and education critics place high expectations on teachers as educators and role models, while teachers are subject to severe criticism when it is felt that they are not preparing students adequately or are failing to meet their mandates (King and Peart, 1992). Many educational reforms are implemented with the assumption that teachers will automatically be prepared to take on new roles, adapt to new curricular demands, or modify their orientations to teaching and learning. In practice, though, teachers require sufficient input, commitment from administrators and peers, background preparation, resource support, and confidence in the efforts of other teachers to reshape their

jobs and work environment before they are likely to engage fully in educational reform processes, even if they support the general directions or
objectives driving those changes. Teachers' associations across Canada are
reporting high levels of stress and frustration among their memberships
associated with an 'overwhelming burden' that periodic modifications in
curriculum, programming, and administrative restructuring have produced along with increased workloads, inadequate preparation time,
insufficient in-service training, larger class sizes, lack of teacher involvement in educational planning, and insufficient communication and support from central administrative bodies (Council of Ministers of
Education Canada, 1996: 14–15).

Several interrelated sets of pressures may intensify the burdens and
stresses felt by teachers when schools struggle to meet the needs of
Aboriginal learners and communities without sufficient preparation,
support, and concern for teachers. First, demographic changes mean that
teachers in many schools and regions will need to be prepared to work
with and address the needs of rising numbers and proportions of
Aboriginal students, including some instances when the majority or all
of the students are of Aboriginal ancestry, and other instances where
these trends complement increasing general diversity in student populations. Second, teachers will be required to act as central agents to deliver
curricular and educational programs that include Aboriginal content,
and to ensure that educational practices are relevant and sensitive to
Aboriginal students they work with. Third, in order to satisfy the
arrangements that may be produced through alternative educational
processes (as outlined in the previous chapter and later in this chapter),
there are prospects for a fundamental reorientation of teachers' work
and teachers' interactions within schools and the communities that they
serve. It is crucial that teachers be committed to and—along with policy-
makers, administrators, community members, and students—centrally
involved in discussions, planning, and co-ordination related to these
educational transformations.

Aboriginal Content in Curricula, Materials, and Programming

Curriculum issues lie at the heart of efforts to understand and improve
the educational status and attainment of Aboriginal people. Despite
improvements, two problems are prominent as recurrent themes in the
literature. First, an absence of courses and content that incorporate First

Nations, Métis, Inuit, and other indigenous people and their histories, values, and cultural practices in many schools perpetuates the gap that many Aboriginal people feel between the dominant culture and their own world. Second, Aboriginal people frequently reiterate concerns that an anti-Aboriginal bias remains in many school materials and pedagogical approaches (Royal Commission on Aboriginal Peoples, 1993: 20).

Some of these trends reveal the deep-rooted legacy of mistrust that has permeated Aboriginal people's relations with the school system following dispiriting or abusive experiences with the residential school system, such as those outlined in Chapter 3, and marginalization within provincial or territorial school settings (Ryan, 1996). This history, combined with increasing public acknowledgement by policy-makers and educators of the necessity of incorporating Aboriginal perspectives and content into school processes, has perhaps contributed to disappointment when rising expectations do not match everyday experiences in the schools. It is not surprising, in this context, that the Royal Commission on Aboriginal Peoples (1996c: 164) observes that, 'For Aboriginal youth, remaining in school can be a lonely, isolating and degrading experience' that is felt even more deeply at the post-secondary level.

Such isolation and marginalization are experienced socially and personally, but they also reflect the absence of opportunities for Aboriginal students to validate their identities and heritage. The impact of these absences can be illustrated through trends that indicate declining knowledge or use of Aboriginal languages, strongly signified by the potential disappearance of many First Nations languages. Out of the more than 50 Aboriginal languages spoken in Canada at the time of European contact, only three—Ojibwa, Cree, and Inuktitut—have a sufficient base from which to ensure their long-term continuity (Norris, 1998).

Several innovative school programs, especially under First Nations control, have been introduced to foster language development, but the extent to which they are offered and available to students is severely constrained (Assembly of First Nations, 1994). Littlejohn and Fredeen (1993: 59, 78) report that fewer than one in five of the schools serving Aboriginal students that they surveyed in Saskatchewan in the late 1980s indicated that they offered any form of First Nations language training in their programs, and many of the Native language programs that did exist were jeopardized by inadequate funding and supporting resources. In a survey of Métis people in Saskatchewan, the Gabriel Dumont Institute (1993: 31) revealed that fewer than one-third of respondents reported that they had encountered Métis studies in either high school or elementary school, while fewer than two out of five had had any Aboriginal studies in elementary school and just under 30 per cent were exposed to Aboriginal studies in high school. Findings from a national survey of schools attended by First Nations students revealed considerable variations in the teaching of Native languages, depending on key factors like grade level and jurisdiction, with just under 30 per cent of high schools, 26.7 per cent of public schools, and 86.9 per cent of band and federal schools reporting that they offered First Nations language instruction (Kirkness and Bowman, 1992: 43). Two parallel reports commissioned for the Royal Commission on Aboriginal Peoples offer similar pessimistic assessments of the state of Aboriginal language instruction in Canadian schools. Fettes and Norton (2000: 49) conclude that schools continue to have a negative impact on Aboriginal language use and transmission, in part because 'No province has expressed a willingness to provide regular instruction through the medium of an Aboriginal language.' Hébert (2000) stresses that, even in situations where a commitment to heritage language instruction has been expressed, Aboriginal language and literacy programs often fail to achieve their aims because of inappropriate teaching methods, curricular materials, and school practices.

Curricular concerns for Aboriginal people extend far beyond language issues. Boredom in general, often induced by irrelevant curricula, is frequently cited in the literature on school dropouts as a cause of early school leaving (Gilbert et al., 1993: 23; Tanner et al., 1995: 20–1). These problems are intensified among Aboriginal youth who see the school as unwelcoming and unreceptive to their own needs and perspectives, or for whom discontinuities between school expectations and their own cultural backgrounds create tensions and adjustment problems (Gabriel Dumont Institute, 1993: 25; Deyhle and Swisher, 1997: 162).

Research findings on curricular barriers are counterpoised with studies that show the benefits of Aboriginal courses and content for students of indigenous heritage. The mere inclusion of Aboriginal perspectives and material in the schooling process is a starting point to improve school retention and performance by Aboriginal students and to foster cross-cultural understanding. Simple exposure to curricula, though, does not in itself guarantee that meaningful outcomes will be produced, since curriculum is only one element of the total school context or environment. Schools that report the greatest success in terms of retention and educational achievement among Aboriginal students tend to be those that incorporate indigenous orientations across the entire range of curricular subjects, school programming, and educational activities (Kehoe and Echols, 1994: 62–3; Haig-Brown et al., 1997; LaFrance, 2000). Culturally appropriate education, viewed in this light, refers not only to the recognition of Aboriginal cultures and heritage in the curriculum, but to approaches that underlie the entire organization and delivery of schooling.

Much success, in these regards, has been achieved so far by schools under First Nations control and by alternative schools operating in or outside of other education systems. The National Indian Brotherhood/ Assembly of First Nations (1988: 77) and the Royal Commission on Aboriginal Peoples (1996c) concur that student learning is best facilitated by holistic approaches to pedagogy, curricula, and culture. Wilson (1994: 309) observes that Aboriginal students respond especially well to learning situations that promote 'active experimentation', highlighting the value of direct experience more than abstract learning situations. More generally, Ryan (1996: 123) emphasizes the strong view among Aboriginal communities that curricular adaptations must be accompanied by more fundamental restructuring of educational frameworks and relationships (discussed later in this chapter) in order to produce meaningful results.

Although it is common to conceptualize curricula and programming as matters of content and pedagogy (in terms of how content is shared or transmitted), it is important to acknowledge as well that education is about transforming people and their relationships with themselves, other people, and the world in general. This is one of the central reasons why First Nations asserted the objective of 'Indian control of Indian education' in 1972 as a central component in their strategy to break free from a colonial legacy to move towards effective self-determination. Education functions in this way not just as a vehicle by which Aboriginal people are able to gain access to opportunities and credentials that have historically been denied to them, but more importantly it becomes a means by which their heritage, identities, and future prospects can be linked together in ways that are meaningful to them.

There are, though, disturbing contradictions associated with this dimension of schooling. We have already examined how individuals are likely to enhance their social and economic opportunities as they gain exposure to and credentials from formal education. Education more generally can be beneficial by enabling people to operate in, and meet the expectations associated with, diverse social circumstances. However, it also contributes to the formation of new identities and characteristics. This reality is often difficult for any group to contend with, but it contains particular dimensions that are especially problematic from an Aboriginal perspective. This is because formal education often stands apart from, and may sometimes actually be in conflict with, standards, expectations, and practices that prevail in the learners' homes and communities.

These potential contradictions have their roots in the nineteenth-century origins of Canada's public school systems. Constitutionally, under the 1867 British North America Act, education for most Canadians was left under provincial jurisdiction, with the expectation that there would be active representation and financing at the school district level, in order to win public support for schooling and to provide some responsiveness to local community concerns (Stamp, 1977: 31–2). However, teachers and education officials also gained increasing authority to set and deliver the curriculum and to discipline children under the guise that parents, churches, and local organizations were often too narrow and parochial in their views and did not always possess the commitment to common social development that public education could offer (McDonald, 1977: 50 ff.; Wotherspoon, 1998: 51–2). Schooling for students legally defined as 'Indians', by contrast, remained under the control of the federal government, which in turn frequently delegated responsibility for the operation of schools to church or, after World War II, to provincial agencies. Although the government adopted various orientations and practices towards Indian education (such as day schools, boarding schools near reserves, or more distant residential or industrial training schools), its major policy orientation, as we have seen, was aimed at the 'assimilation' of children of Aboriginal ancestry (Barman et al., 1986), if not cultural genocide. Efforts to separate indigenous children from their parents, kin networks, and cultural heritage were prominent tools in the pursuit of assimilation objectives.

More broadly, the socially inclusive nature of public schooling, with its commitment to foster general values and serve people from diverse social backgrounds, remains an important dimension of public education systems. Despite criticisms from selected interests, public schooling retains a strong core of general support relative to private schooling alternatives that are more likely to be driven by the interests of a narrower range of the population (Kachur, 1999: 140–1). However, within schooling an integrative orientation can sometimes obscure crucial processes that in practice exclude specific groups of students or devalue their families and backgrounds. In these regards, parallel to the residential schooling experience, public schools often give a privileged though unquestioned place to knowledge, expectations, attitudes, and behaviour that are not only different from, but hostile to, those associated with the students' heritage.

These relationships have significance at two levels. While they attend school, students are likely to experience discomfort and uncertainty with aspects of the schooling process, dissociation from family or community members, or more general anxiety over these divergent experiences. For those who complete schooling, their status as persons who have been educated in a 'white' institution, especially at higher levels, may produce incongruities between their new identities and their home communities. It is important, therefore, to consider carefully the relationship between schooling and the communities that schools serve, as well as to ask questions about what it means, both for individuals and for their relations with others, to be educated.

ALTERNATIVE CONCEPTIONS AND FORMS OF EDUCATION

The emergence of the 'knowledge society' has given renewed centrality to the importance of formal education to social advancement, but it has also drawn attention to diverse educational forms that take place outside of formal schooling. Livingstone (1999) describes the depths of hidden 'icebergs' of learning that occur in homes, workplaces, community settings, and other sites as people expand their interests or seek information that allows them to manage basic life needs, cope with changing technologies, keep abreast of social and employment-related challenges, learn about other cultures or their own place in the world, or expand their horizons and options for the future. A growing range of adult education programs, employment training initiatives, entrepreneurial development incentives, and labour market entry programs for youth and adults is being offered by First Nations, federal and provincial governments, community agencies, and private and joint sources. These programs range from life skills and basic education courses to short-term job training ventures and transition programs to facilitate entry into formal certificate, diploma, or degree studies. In addition to these options, evidence suggests that substantial proportions of Aboriginal children and adults, like the population as a whole, are engaged at least several hours every week in informal learning ventures characterized by intentional efforts, individually or collectively, to learn new knowledge related to work, home, personal, or community matters (Livingstone, 2000; Wotherspoon and Butler, 1999). In all of these endeavours, people are gaining knowledge and education beyond what is commonly recognized for credit or credentials. These trends have mixed implications. They reveal substantial educational resources that may facilitate additional learning in both formal and informal settings and provide sources of knowledge and capabilities that may promote further growth and advancement for individuals, communities, and organizations over and above levels that are normally assumed to prevail. However, Livingstone (1999: 30–1) cautions that educational inequality and privilege may be reproduced both in and beyond these informal settings as those with the highest levels of formal education are best situated to take advantage of non-formal education and training opportunities and to translate their informal learning into assets recognized by employers, educational bodies, or other agencies.

One of the major educational forms of significance for Aboriginal people and their orientations to conventional education systems is indigenous knowledge. Indigenous knowledge has received little or no attention until recently in general educational discussions and planning, due to a general Eurocentric bias in state-sponsored education combined with the more deliberate historical efforts by churches, state institutions, and other agents to undermine or eradicate Aboriginal culture. Colonization processes become successful, in part, when dominant groups privilege their own value and knowledge systems, ignoring, denying any validity to, or dismissing as primitive those associated with the group being colonized. Indigenous culture, heritage, and knowledge have been excluded or left on the margins of educational practice through the assimilationist emphasis of missionary-led education, residential schooling, and public schooling. However, while many Aboriginal people have had little connection with or have chosen to distance themselves from indigenous knowledge, Aboriginal ways of knowing and teaching have survived to a point that they are gaining renewed attention and status.

There are at least three major reasons for the emergence of contemporary interest in indigenous knowledge. First, accompanying Aboriginal peoples' struggles in Canada and other nations to achieve decolonization is a growing consciousness of and appreciation for their distinct heritage and approaches to the world. This is significant both to guard against further loss of traditions, languages, relationships, and knowledge and to strengthen vision, identity, and vitality among Aboriginal people and their communities. It has taken several decades since the removal of Indian Act regulations and guidelines to prohibit the practice of ceremonies and the transmission of other cultural forms for the emergence in many circumstances of an atmosphere conducive to celebrate Aboriginal heritage, share the teachings of the Elders, and appreciate indigenous ways of knowing.

Second, a circumstance has arisen parallel to the recognition of Aboriginal rights and the increasing respect for the validity of indigenous knowledge, and that is a series of threats by non-Aboriginal interests seeking to appropriate or gain control over selective information for their own profit or other purposes. While public controversies over ownership, control, and use of Aboriginal art and artifacts have arisen periodically in this regard, recent concern is mounting in Canada and internationally over indigenous peoples' rights and abilities to honour and regulate knowledge, practices, and intellectual ownership in areas like ecology, biological diversity, medicine, healing, and spirituality (Battiste and Henderson, 2000; UN Working Group on Indigenous Populations, 1994; Research and Analysis Directorate, Department of Indian Affairs and Northern Development, 1999).

Third, interest in Aboriginal knowledge or epistemologies has accompanied what is often portrayed as 'the post-modernist politics of difference', in which diverse social groups have asserted their demands for recognition of rights and for policies to address specified collective needs. These movements reject European-based models of organization and thought grounded in rational, scientific, or bureaucratic principles. They stress their need for alternative ways of understanding and interacting with the world and their need for effective responses to forms of decision-making and practice they experience as oppressive, destructive, and undemocratic (Graveline, 1998; Prince and Rice, 2000).

These challenges have created opportunities for the promotion and recognition of Aboriginal or indigenous knowledge as part of an established, distinct way of understanding, teaching about, and engaging with the world in social, spiritual, and material senses. While there are distinctions in the nature and forms of Aboriginal knowledge and the practices associated with it, common foundations appear across quite diverse indigenous societies. Regardless of its specific manifestations, indigenous knowledge encompasses established ways of knowing, forms of knowl-

edge, and pedagogical practices. Several educators and scholars have outlined the central dimensions of indigenous epistemologies, both to
demonstrate their status and validity as established knowledge forms and
as a means of promoting their application and of ensuring their guidance
in the development of educational practice by and for Aboriginal people
(see, e.g., Battiste, 2000; Cajete, 1999). Battiste and Henderson (2000:
35–6), however, caution against efforts to specify and codify indigenous
knowledge too firmly, especially when it is defined or understood from a
Western or Eurocentric perspective: first, because indigenous knowledge
does not fit into preconceived notions of culture; second, because of its
diversity; and third, because it is rooted in practical activity and social
relationships rather than something that is abstract and separate from the
learner or knower. The Royal Commission on Aboriginal Peoples (1996c:
526–7) summarizes many of these points, acknowledging indigenous or
traditional knowledge as:

> a discrete system of knowledge with its own philosophical and value
> base. Aboriginal peoples hold the belief that traditional knowledge
> derives from the Creator and is spiritual in essence. It includes ecologi-
> cal teachings, medical knowledge, common attitudes toward Mother
> Earth and the Circle of Life, and a sense of kinship with all creatures.
>
> Each nation also has its own body of knowledge that encompasses
> language, belief systems, ways of thinking and behaving, ceremonies,
> stories, dances and history . . . . [However] the gatekeepers of western
> intellectual traditions have repeatedly dismissed traditional knowledge
> as inconsequential and unfounded . . . .
>
> Traditional knowledge also has its forms of transmission . . . . While
> elders do not reject participation in Canadian education, they question
> the exclusion of traditional knowledge and its methods of transmission
> . . . [and] when they try to become involved in the education process,
> they find many obstacles.

The challenge for educators, policy-makers, and those who rely on
schooling to meet training and accreditation needs is to ensure appropriate recognition and places for Aboriginal knowledge within educational
programming at the same time that they do not usurp, undermine, or
alter the role of Elders and other Aboriginal people to determine and
share appropriate knowledge forms within their own community and
cultural contexts.

.

ABORIGINAL LEARNERS AND THE CONSTRUCTION
OF NOTIONS OF RISK AND RESILIENCE

One of the ways in which educational practices and relationships are being reconceptualized is evident in recent applications of the notion of 'risk' by educators, social service providers, and policy-makers to selected groups of children and youth. The 'at-risk' label has been employed with increasing frequency to refer to categories of learners who appear to have higher than average prospects of leaving school prior to high school completion or of exhibiting other serious behavioural or developmental problems later in life. While definitions and characteristics associated with risk vary, children and youth most likely to be considered 'at risk' include visible minorities, persons living in poverty, residents of inner-city and less developed rural regions, those who do not speak the dominant school language fluently, children from single-parent families, and Aboriginal people (Guy, 1997; OECD, 1998: 5–6). It is evident that Aboriginal children and youth, in addition to being identified as a high-risk group in their own right, frequently are located in several other risk categories simultaneously.

Attentiveness to students at risk has the advantage of prompting the introduction of resources, services, or programming that may be necessary to improve the chances for educational progress or success among students with particular needs or difficulties. However, there are several dangers or limitations contained within the language and practices associated with at-risk learners. In particular, the tendency to focus on specific individuals or categories of the population can create or reinforce negative stereotypes, placing undue attention on attributes or behaviour viewed officially as undesirable. In other words, as with self-fulfilling prophesies, educators and policy-makers sometimes act in ways that produce, rather than address, real problems (Fine, 1993: 104–5; Natriello et al., 1990: 3). It must be kept in mind, as well, that nearly all children and youth experience life circumstances, however temporary, that may signify them as at risk and that significant proportions of those in high-risk categories do complete school and engage in other life transitions successfully (Wotherspoon and Schissel, 2000: 6). For these reasons, some commentators have begun to focus attention on notions of 'resilience', which shift emphasis from alleged deficits or problems in the learner to factors that enable some students to succeed despite adversity (Jenkins and Keating, 1998; Wang et al., 1998).

Regardless of what language or focus is employed with respect to so-called 'problem' categories of learners and their prospects, it is essential that arrangements and practices that characterize schooling are linked with a thorough understanding of the community and social contexts within which schooling takes place. Educators often adopt language and employ practices that, despite their supposed neutrality, contain hidden assumptions and prescriptions that can disadvantage particular student groups. Cummins (1986: 21) argues that the extent to which students from minority backgrounds are either 'disabled' or 'empowered' through schooling is a consequence of the degree to which four institutional characteristics are incorporated into educational practices: minority languages and cultures; participation by community members; pedagogy that promotes active involvement on the part of minority students; and assessment measures that avoid viewing the source of problems experienced by minority students as residing in the students themselves or in their cultures. Even testing processes that are presumed to be neutral indicators of student achievement in fact involve cultural processes that are incongruent with Aboriginal students' expectations and experiences (Deyhle, 1986: 386–7). One of the most powerful forms of school control often leading to marginalization and withdrawal is silencing, in which students are denied opportunities to voice their concerns or to examine issues of importance to them, or where students are made to feel that their interests and experiences are subordinate or marginal to what is considered to be the 'real' business of learning (Wotherspoon, 1998: 95). Consequently, it is essential that schooling implement such practices as the full integration of teachers, programming, and curricular content that arise from or are grounded in the students' social and community contexts in order to establish a basis on which students and their concerns can be addressed through the educational process.

EDUCATIONAL GOVERNANCE AND RESOURCES

The organization, administration, and financing of education do not contribute directly to learning processes, but they establish limitations and possibilities for what happens in schools as well as for educational outcomes. Foremost among concerns whereby educational resources and governance can affect educational performance by Aboriginal students are (1) the presence of educational administrators and school personnel who understand and are sympathetic to indigenous perspectives and concerns, (2) the provision of sufficient resources and planning frameworks to address real educational needs, and (3) mechanisms to ensure meaningful participation by Aboriginal people in all aspects of the educational process (Mills Consulting, 1993: 19–20; Saskatchewan Education, 1991: 7; National Indian Brotherhood/Assembly of First Nations, 1988: 75–6). The establishment of band-controlled schooling within First Nations jurisdictions has addressed some of these issues, but considerable improvements are required in the linkages between schools and communities in both band-controlled and provincial/territorial school systems.

Much of the recent analysis of educational governance and participation in decision-making has been to clarify objectives and strategies to achieve the long-standing First Nations objective of 'Indian control of Indian education' (see, e.g., Battiste and Barman, 1995; Catellano et al., 2000).While there is consensus over the importance of incorporating Aboriginal materials and perspectives into the curriculum, there is considerable debate over the meaning, nature, and consequences of First Nations control over education. As a result, a diverse and often widely fragmented range of educational goals and programming alternatives has emerged in recent years. In some cases, this has resulted in parallel education systems, with initiatives oriented to full, direct governance by First Nations over education placed alongside conventional education systems, which in turn must address pressures to modify existing programs and services or create a variety of alternative educational delivery mechanisms. Ryan (1995: 225–6), making reference to post-secondary education but in a manner that applies also to elementary and secondary schooling, outlines three alternative models that should be considered as possible responses to ensure responsiveness to the learning concerns of indigenous students: (1) the incorporation into mainstream schooling programs of compensatory measures for Aboriginal students who experience educational difficulties; (2) the implementation of a range of alternative arrangements within school systems to provide flexibility in time and space in order to accommodate diverse student needs; and (3) the adoption of Aboriginal-controlled education systems built upon fundamental changes to educational structures and programming. Even where First Nations governance has been accomplished, there are considerable variations in the forms that such control takes, how it operates, and how effective it is (Hampton and Wolfson, 1994: 92–5; Paquette, 1989; Royal Commission on Aboriginal Peoples, 1996c).

The growing proliferation of educational alternatives and programs, combined with the continuing 'education gap' experienced by many Aboriginal people, points to a need for educators, researchers, and policy-makers to investigate carefully how educational governance, educational processes, and educational outcomes affect one another. It is important, in this analysis, to gain a sense of what works, what doesn't work, and what issues are not being addressed because they fall between jurisdictions or beyond the range of concerns that specific schools or agencies are preoccupied with.

It is clear that the development of effective strategies to arrange and deliver education in such a way as to improve retention, involvement, and performance by Aboriginal pupils will require both new resources and the reallocation of existing services and resources. Effective responses to these concerns require labour-intensive efforts by educational planners and administrators, teachers, and community members to ensure that they produce more than superficial or piecemeal changes to selected areas of educational practice. As was noted in the previous chapter with respect to Aboriginal students' perceptions of their own educational experiences, there is satisfaction with, and faith in, many dimensions of the schooling process. Nonetheless, the most effective schools and programs are ones that adopt an orientation far different from prevailing practices in many conventional classrooms, ensuring continuing sensitivity to the kinds of environment and practices that accept and build upon students' needs, lives, and potential futures.

Paradoxically, demands for these changes are intensifying within a period of state and educational reform driven in significant ways by demands to limit state funding and to control or restrict the services offered by schools and other public agencies. Challenges are emerging from conflicting social vantage points and ideological positions. As education takes on growing value as a commodity in the 'knowledge economy', there is a tendency for people to become increasingly vocal in their demands for the kinds of education and training that will pay them the dividends they seek or expect. These expressions take several forms, including calls for accountability, consumer choice, improvements in the standards and quality of education, more relevant training for current labour markets, better discipline and security, and responsiveness to particular constituencies of parents or cultural groups (Wotherspoon, 1998: 196 ff.). While public debate over education is an ongoing and essential feature of schooling in democratic societies, there is a danger when schools are called upon to meet too many different expectations, particularly when the resources to meet those demands are in jeopardy. This is complicated by recent market-based reforms in social policy, leading to reduced public spending, pressure to create private alternatives, and a business orientation in education, health care, and other social services established to serve diverse public functions (Taylor, 2001).

These trends in many ways are intensified with respect to public services oriented to Aboriginal populations. Hylton (1999: 79, 87) observes that Aboriginal people are likely to be 'disproportionately affected by the problems that social programs are intended to address' at the same time that many such programs have insufficient resources in the first place and are further jeopardized by additional funding constraints, restructuring, or limited guidelines. These arrangements have posed special challenges for the complete development of effective First Nations control of education in regard to both specific schooling arrangements and broader self-government frameworks. Among the major concerns are federally imposed restrictions on the terms, time frame, and conditions of funding (making it difficult to engage in and follow through on long-term planning), insufficient flexibility in the way that resources are allocated, competing priorities, and pressing needs for services and programs that exceed the amount of available funding (Brady, 1991; Burns, 1998; Subcommittee on Aboriginal Education, 1996). Although some of these problems are unique to the arrangements concerning the establishment, financing, and regulation of band control, many of them are shared with provincial or territorial schools as shifts occur in the relations among provincial governments, municipalities, or school boards in terms of school finance, regulation, and planning in various jurisdictions across Canada. These changes have meant that, even where some consensus emerges around the need to address Aboriginal students' and programming needs, the capacity to meet those challenges may be hindered by competing priorities, organizational uncertainty or restructuring, and insufficient resources.

COMMUNITY FACTORS

What happens in, and as a consequence of, schooling is shaped by more than features strictly internal to education systems. As we have observed, schools must acknowledge the impact of orientations, concerns, and predispositions that educational participants bring with them into the school, along with the community, political, and socio-economic environments in which the schools operate. For these reasons, a prominent theme in research and policy statements concerned with improving educational circumstances for Aboriginal people is apparent in demands for stronger co-operation between parents and schools, and increased involvement in the schools by parents, Elders, and other community members.

The cultivation of school-community relationships can contribute to open communication, mutual respect, and new understandings that may enhance educational environments and processes. It is equally important through these relationships for school personnel and schooling arrangements to take into account the realities and concerns that confront those served by schools in their everyday experiences (Royal Commission on Aboriginal Peoples, 1993: 20, 23; Saskatchewan Education, 1996: 6). Community and cultural concerns, presented this way, reflect both an ongoing dialogue between school personnel, parents, Elders, and other community members about the expectations and goals of education, as framed in conventional ways, as well as about the potential contributions that schooling could make to individual and community futures conceived in much broader ways.

Effective educational practice, in these respects, requires an understanding of how socio-economic conditions affect people at both individual and community levels. The absence of job opportunities in a community, for instance, presents conflicting challenges for schools. When people have a sense that their options are limited, individuals may be disinclined to take an active interest in completing their schooling, inducing the potential for such serious concerns as poverty, crime, substance abuse, family breakdown, loss of infrastructural support services, and other serious problems to become widespread. Conversely, individuals may employ schooling and educational opportunities as vehicles to escape from circumstances they see as undesirable or limiting. To the extent that education channels young people out of communities that require renewal and vitality, schools may contribute to the further disintegration of small communities or they may be viewed by local community members as intrusive forces that contribute little to further development except the opportunities that select individuals are able to benefit from. Moreover, migration out of or back to home communities and reserves as a result of parents' pursuit of work or educational opportunities means that children may experience disruptions in learning and adjustment to new environments (Ryan, 1995: 223–4).

Social and economic problems, in turn, affect learning practices and outcomes both directly and indirectly. Poverty, for instance, increases the risk of hunger and nutritional disorders, low self-esteem, ill health, attention deficits, and repeated school absences, among other problems. These, in turn, contribute to lowered educational achievements and increased chances of dropping out of school (Hess, 1989: 5–7). Levin and Riffel (1997: 117) observe that:

> Poor economic status is associated with weaker preparation before entering school, less support for students in school, and disruptions such as hunger, family violence, and mobility. Low socio-economic status is more strongly associated with poor educational outcomes than any other variable. Yet educators are quite ambivalent about the meaning of poverty for their work and the conduct of schooling.

Children whose parents have low levels of education and income are among the students most likely to leave school before graduation (Gilbert et al., 1993: 23; Gilbert and Frank, 1998). Moreover, insofar as Aboriginal people continue to experience higher than average rates of poverty, unemployment, and similar socio-economic problems, they repeatedly encounter negative stereotypes and racism that further contribute to difficulties in achieving positive self-esteem and greater levels of educational and occupational success (Ponting, 1998: 280–2). Furniss (1999) describes the negative impact of 'common-sense' racism in a northern British Columbia community where neither teachers nor administrators identified racial discrimination as a serious educational issue, in contrast to widespread concern over the phenomenon by Aboriginal students and family members.

At the same time, media attention and public concern about issues like youth crime, delinquency, alcohol and drug abuse, AIDS, and street culture have reinforced negative portrayals of youth, frequently targeting those of Aboriginal ancestry as marginalized and unfocused; these images divert attention away from an analysis of the sources of these serious problems, thereby compounding them through an absence of effective interventions, services, and solutions (Royal Commission on Aboriginal Peoples, 1993: 40–2; Schissel, 1997).

Consideration of the problems cited above must be tempered with our awareness that Aboriginal people, like the general population, do not constitute a homogeneous group. They live in diverse circumstances, shaped by history, region, gender, class, legal distinctions, and other factors (Satzewich and Wotherspoon, 2000). What this means for schooling and the analysis of educational issues is that acknowledgement of 'difference', based on cultural and social factors, must take into consideration how experiences vary within Aboriginal populations as well as between Aboriginal people and the general population. While a frank assessment of disruptive and often serious problems is necessary where these apply to specific individuals and communities, this cannot be to the detriment of recognizing that Aboriginal realities rarely match the stereotypical conceptions of them. Several researchers emphasize the repeated coexistence of commitment among Aboriginal parents to widely held mainstream educational values, like the desire for their children to perform well in school, to complete high school, and to be prepared for entry into the labour force, with more specific aspirations that they develop a sense of self-esteem, pride in their heritage, and validation of their backgrounds as indigenous people (see, e.g., Kehoe and Echols, 1994: 62; Castellano et al., 2000: 253).

For Aboriginal children, like other students, school performance is enhanced by active parental support and encouragement to succeed, and is reinforced by facilitative services and environments. Schools and educational policy-makers at all levels must be committed to the development of measures to ensure that schooling embraces these diverse needs and interests, in large part through open relations and continuing dialogue with parents and other members of the communities they are intended to serve.

SUMMARY

Several factors within schools, in conjunction with students' lives and experiences along with the community and socio-economic and political environments connected to schooling, contribute to variable prospects for educational success or failure among Aboriginal people. It is crucial not to attend exclusively to the individual, the culture, or any other single level or set of factors when attempting to understand and take action to address educational problems or failure. Teachers, schools, and educational programs that are receptive to the perspectives, contributions, and social circumstances of Aboriginal people are more likely to produce positive results than those that fail to acknowledge these concerns. In this respect, the literature and assessments of specific cases reveal that educational strategies that tend to be most effective in overcoming many of the educational gaps that remain between Aboriginal and non-Aboriginal people are those that adopt an integrated approach. These factors, as we have seen, are echoed in the responses of the students themselves. Curiously, despite movement to incorporate an Aboriginal presence into educational practice and research, the voices of indigenous children and youth have remained relatively silent in most investigations of schooling. Our intention in the work at hand has been to take a small step towards remedying this lacuna.

QUESTIONS FOR CRITICAL THOUGHT

1. Discuss the extent to which educational success or failure, in general and with specific reference to Aboriginal people, is a consequence of in-school factors as opposed to out-of-school factors.
2. Discuss the importance of culture and language programs for Aboriginal education.
3. How have federal government funding and public debates about funding affected educational prospects for Aboriginal people in Canada?
4. What are the main themes or concerns in the literature on schooling experiences of Aboriginal children and youth? How does each of these factors contribute to educational success or failure? What other factors must be considered in the analysis of these educational outcomes?
5. Discuss the role that teachers play in educational experiences and outcomes for Aboriginal children and youth. What are some of the factors that limit teachers' ability to be as effective as they would like? How can schooling be changed to make teachers more effective?
6. What is the difference between formal and informal learning? To what extent, and in what ways, could greater formal recognition of informal learning contribute to educational improvement?
7. What is indigenous knowledge? What is the relationship between formal schooling and indigenous knowledge? Discuss the extent to which indigenous knowledge could or should be part of regular school curricula and programming.

RECOMMENDED READING

Federation of Saskatchewan Indian Nations. 1999. *Saskatchewan and Aboriginal Peoples in the 21st Century: Social, Economic and Political Changes and Challenges.* Regina: PrintWest Publishing.

The report details the current socio-economic and political circumstances and future prospects for Aboriginal people in Saskatchewan. While educational practices are not the central focus, the study documents the close interconnections among demographic trends, economic change, and key institutional sectors, and the implications of this interconnectedness for both Aboriginal and non-Aboriginal populations.

Frideres, James S. 2000. *Aboriginal Peoples in Canada: Contemporary Conflicts*, 5th edn. Scarborough, Ont.: Prentice-Hall Allyn and Bacon.

Frideres presents a comprehensive overview of the history and current conditions of Aboriginal peoples in relation to other groups in Canada. He profiles educational conditions for Canada's Native peoples in conjunction with other areas of social, economic, and political life. Interpretation of historical and legal frameworks provides a basis for considering the future prospects of self-government and Aboriginal representation in mainstream institutional settings.

Kirkness, Verna, and Sheena Selkirk Bowman. 1992. *First Nations and Schools: Triumphs and Struggles*. Toronto: Canadian Education Association.

The authors offer a useful summary of innovations and challenges confronting schools in their efforts to make schooling more relevant for and representative of Aboriginal people. Based on a survey of developments in First Nations education, the book provides data and examples drawn from jurisdictions throughout Canada, as well as brief overviews of educational history and First Nations visions of education.

Subcommittee on Aboriginal Education. 1996. *Sharing the Knowledge: The Path to Success and Equal Opportunities in Education*. Report of the Standing Committee on Aboriginal Affairs and Northern Development. Ottawa: Canada Comunications Group.

The report is useful as a summary of major educational concerns, initiatives, and possibilities.

CHAPTER 6

❖

EDUCATION, JUSTICE, AND COMMUNITY: A PARADIGM FOR ENFRANCHISING CHILDREN AND YOUTH

INTRODUCTION

From our exploration of several educational/cultural programs that respond to the historical and contemporary plight of Aboriginal children in a Euro-Canadian educational system, we are aware that their success stories are characterized by a rather fundamental paradigm shift in educational thinking: that for education to be truly an instrument of social justice and social redress—along with its formal function of intellectual development—it must discard the hierarchical disciplinary form and replace it with a model of individual or communal self-determination. In essence, the educational/community models described in the last two chapters work because they struggle to democratize education at its very core by realizing that true mentoring can occur only in a non-threatening, non-authoritarian context and that any learner, despite age, needs to seek learning and not have it thrust upon him/her.

Interestingly, another basic fact of these non-abusive schools is that they are not driven by fiscal obsession. Although they do struggle to find enough money to operate, they make do with what they have and rely on the intrinsic wealth provided by dedicated staff and students. Their philosophy about money is simple and profound: schools are never to be considered an expense. Quite clearly in this philosophy, the moment education and fiscal responsibility are discussed in the same context, students become reduced to commodities in which production is based on fixed inputs. The discourse that includes education and public spending in the same breath necessarily dehumanizes children and youth.

ALTERNATIVE EDUCATION AS A PARADIGM FOR SOCIAL JUSTICE

Alternative models of dealing with children and youth are responsive to the needs of students from a variety of socio-cultural settings. They most often adjust to the needs of students who are economically disadvantaged and who often lack the day-to-day supports that all persons require. Such schools provide for the educational, social, and personal needs of students who do not fit easily or well into the system of standardized education. Typically, the students in these schools have levels of achievement that would be considered inadequate in traditional educational systems. The successes of the schools we have studied indicate that a flexible, more holistic system of learning is viable, appropriate, and amazingly successful for students who would otherwise 'fall through the cracks'. Schools such as Won Ska and Princess Alexandria, described previously in this book, attest to the importance of providing an educational context that is relevant to the lives of the least privileged children and youth.

We believe that the policies and practices that frame these alternative school programs should frame all educational models. School systems that take steps to integrate the vast intellectual, social, cultural, and geographic differences encompassed by their students in the process will be providing superior educational contexts for all students. And, we use some of the outstanding successes in public alternative schools to make this point, keeping in mind the alternative justice practised in these innovative schools, especially First Nations healing models for youth.

However, for alternative educational approaches to be successful, there must be, as well, a broadening of understanding about the multiple competencies that students inevitably bring with them that may be developed through schooling and other life experiences. McGinty (1999: 136–7), for instance, contrary to assumptions that students with multiple stresses in their lives always do poorly in school, found that female students with considerable family responsibilities develop a strength or 'toughness' that can be transferred to school success. Opening educators' awareness to students' unconventional learning need not lead to academic under-achievement. Schools that adopt high expectations, rather than reduced standards, are repeatedly observed to produce more positive outcomes among minority students and other groups of at-risk learners (Gaskell, 1995: 278–9; Kehoe and Echols, 1994: 62–4; Renihan et al., 1994: 98). Moreover, we have noted earlier that research on informal learning suggests that students from all backgrounds, and especially those from cultural minorities and less privileged circumstances, have strong capabilities that are not acknowledged or are even undermined in conventional school situations (Livingstone, 1999; Wotherspoon and Butler, 1999). The following description (Schissel, 1997) illustrates how one inner-city elementary school in Saskatoon attends to the life contingencies of its students by recognizing the resiliency of a student who would otherwise be considered high-risk:

> this program demonstrates the inherent goodness in children despite the hatred and mistrust we see in the media. Principal Schmidt, for example, talks of instances in which an Elder['s] child has come to school out of control and verbally abusive; as the staff examines the roots of this behaviour, it is often found that the student's parents or guardians have been drinking and fighting all night, the student has to make breakfast for his or her siblings and get them off to school and then has to get him or herself ready for school, all the while observing or experiencing abuse and neglect. When framed in this context, the achievements of the student are remarkable, responsible, and benevolent by any standard. The school is prepared to treat such kids with the respect and tolerance they deserve, especially given their outstanding display of responsibility in the face of extreme adversity. The school, in turn, makes every effort to place siblings in the same classes or at least to provide them with opportunities to see each other, given the importance of family and caring that children often demonstrate.

That diverse knowledge and capabilities are often ignored is true, as well, in the wider community, where social and cultural resources such as the presence of Aboriginal Elders or individuals with special skills or life histories are often ignored or not represented as legitimate learning resources. Attentiveness to the diversity and richness of the backgrounds that students experience allows educational administrators to focus on learning-related difficulties in relation to the need for basic survival or life skills, or hot lunch programs, rather than seeing these factors as merely related to deprivation or absences in students' and families' lives.

THE IMPORTANCE OF DIVERSE CLIMATES AND PRACTICES WITHIN SCHOOL

By acknowledging the need for linkages between schools and community, we must not lose sight of what schools themselves can do. Many schools have demonstrated effectiveness in attracting students, improving attendance and graduation rates, and fostering other positive outcomes. Such outcomes are made possible through concerted efforts to demon-

strate positive leadership, school climates characterized by equity and sta-
bility, and variety in instruction and management practised by skilled
teachers (Druian and Butler, 1999). Alternative schools that combine a
deliberate 'culture of noticing and caring' with a philosophy of personal
responsibility contribute markedly to student success (Gregory, 1995:
150). Terms like 'spirit of caring', 'warmth and openness', and an 'ethos of
belonging and support' pervade descriptions of schools that are hailed as
effective in promoting success among their students and the communities
they are situated within (see, e.g., Archibald and Haig-Brown, 1995;
Maguire and McAlpine, 1995).

EDUCATION, JUSTICE, AND COMMUNITY

As we attempt to envision a new paradigm for education, it is important
to realize that education is closely connected to social justice and egali-
tarianism. An example of a typical educational model premised on pre-
cepts of collective justice and equality is described in *Making the Spirit
Dance Within: Joe Duquette High School and an Aboriginal Community*
(Haig-Brown et al., 1997). This groundbreaking work is a study of an
alternative inner-city school in Saskatoon whose student body is primarily of First Nations ancestry. Many of the students at the school are 'high-
risk' in that they are disaffiliated from family and community and are relatively susceptible to confrontations with the legal system. The mandate,
as a result, is to provide a democratic, fair environment in which students
can find safety, tolerance, egalitarian treatment, and a non-judgemental,
non-punitive place to stay and learn, at least during the day. And, significantly, the school is conducted within a spiritual/cultural context that
frames the day-to-day activities of the students and staff.

In essence, what the school attempts to do is create an adult-like world
in which autonomy, responsibility, respect, and enfranchisement are the
cornerstones. To do this, the school staff creates an atmosphere of mutual
respect and equality by being reflective about their own behaviour and by
demonstrating respectfulness categorically. Teachers model the types of
conduct they expect in their students by apologizing when necessary, and
by respecting the privacy of the students against other teachers and against
the outside world. At times, this entails not 'ratting' on a student to other
teachers or the principal, and making the school a sanctuary against the
outside, especially from the police. Although the school does co-operate
with the law in terms of alternative measures, it does not allow the law to

intrude into the sanctuary of the school. Further, the atmosphere of community is fostered by a philosophy in which the school belongs to everyone; the symbols of authority and 'pulling rank' are minimized. The school does not have a staff room; when the staff meet, they do so in full view of the entire school community and decisions about the continuance of a student are made collectively.

Despite the fact that Joe Duquette High School is an innovative, community-oriented school, like all schools it necessarily has to draw the line at extreme behaviour. It does not, however, use punishment or intimidation to handle extreme situations. Regarding issues of bullying and violence, the violating student is given a choice: either make the effort to apologize and convince the victim that he or she will be safe from now on, or leave. Given that school is the only safe haven from the world and the last resort for some students, reparation is often the outcome. Expulsion does, however, occur. In keeping with the philosophy of community and mutual investment in the school, students who are expelled are welcomed back when they are ready to accept the community standards. Once again, choice and respect, not punishment, are the baselines. While there are problems to overcome, the school has managed to provide a respectful, egalitarian environment in which punishment is absent and in which teachers are active role models for the kinds of behaviour they expect. Issues of racism, sexism, and class discrimination, which are common in most schools, become subsumed under the umbrella of respect for persons as individuals. And, when treated like real persons, the students respond.

It is quite clear that Joe Duquette High School provides an example of the kind of mutuality that needs to occur between education and social justice. Alternative schools, in their mandates to provide alternative measures to the justice system, strive to promote egalitarian, non-authoritarian relationships with adults (essentially figures of authority) and interdependency instead of abject dependency. Students have a good deal of latitude in decisions about themselves, the curriculum, and extent of their relationships with adults. The 'top-down' relationships that youth in trouble with the law receive in the justice system, for example, are replaced with non-punitive, 'social/professional' alliances that provide young people with the mentoring to become responsible adults. A blending of alternative education and law takes the legal system away from punishment and into the realm of healing. As courts become overburdened with Young Offenders Act cases and as closed-custody institutions are filled, it is obvious that effective alternatives to punishment as incarceration are needed now within the justice system. These alternatives must be connected to healing and education.

At a very basic level, schools like the one described above provide a real community for formerly disconnected students. Community is fundamental to Aboriginal-based education systems and Joe Duquette School provides an example of how schools can serve as surrogate communities, especially in urban centres. In isolated rural centres, on the other hand, the concept of community is no less important but it derives from an already existing cultural solidarity and tradition. Ryan (1995) describes how the Dene community of Lac La Martre in the Northwest Territories has fused culture, education, and justice into a singular cosmology that focuses on formal education, cultural apprenticeship, and a collective morality. Most importantly, the Dene community at Lac La Martre has organized a Community Education Committee to ensure that formal education of both children and adults coincides with the cultural and physical needs of a highly subsistence-based community. The Community Education Committee, which grew, in part, out of the findings of Ryan's participatory action research, has recommended to the community that it refashion the education system to make the Dogrib language a priority in school and in the community. Further, the community, on the advice of the Committee, is implementing cultural instruction by Elders in school and extending the classroom to the land, where instruction by Elders and by formal teachers continues in extended field trips. Constant Elder-youth contact is envisioned as a fundamental education vehicle, and the maintenance of the Dogrib language is the framework around which such education is built.

The traditional community in Lac La Martre, with its focus on holistic education, culture/language, and community, is not unlike the urban alternative school that tries to blend cultural learning, formal learning, and a sense of connectedness. The philosophies and priorities are the same, although the external and internal environments are different. It appears, nonetheless, that despite geography, the things that make education a holistic exercise that prepares students for more than just the world of work are very basic and transferable to all life contexts.

POLICY IMPLICATIONS OF THE STUDY

Our research has sought the opinions of Aboriginal children and youth with respect to their school experiences and their understandings of what constitutes a desirable school environment. Based on their singular and collective sentiments, we here outline policy implications that address central social, cultural, and educational needs of students. These recommendations emphasize the interrelationships between schooling and the social context within which it operates, going beyond curricular changes to address at the same time larger issues of well-being, school governance, and physical and emotional safety.

Recommendation 1: Racism and Discrimination

While schools may have zero-tolerance policies on racism and discrimination, the best schools publicize the principles of understanding of and a compassion for difference on an ongoing basis. The alternative high school in which the talking circles for our research were conducted made a concerted effort to incorporate problems of intolerance and discrimination into its curriculum and into regular talking circles. The students in this setting are constantly reminded of how racism and discrimination, in overt and subtle ways, steal into everyone's life inside and outside school. Furthermore, the teachers constantly discuss how issues of discrimination are to be handled. The constant reminders for staff and students create an ongoing awareness of how prejudice and racism damage individuals. Given the recurrences of these problems as reported by students in our research, our recommendation emphasizes the importance of not letting the issues die at the formal zero-tolerance policy level. Without becoming an institution of policing, schools are at their best when they visit issues of discrimination on a continual but sensitive basis among all staff and students.

Recommendation 2: Time Flexibility

Given that many students express how time commitments outside the school make it difficult to meet the time requirements of attendance and assignments in school, the best schools, both alternative and mainstream, deal with lateness in a less punitive way than has been practised in the past. Moreover, where possible, the best schools adjust the time requirements based on individual need and the exigencies of the lives of the students outside school. Too often, students leave school or are asked to leave based on their inability or unwillingness to meet the time requirements of the formal school curriculum.

Recommendation 3: Cultural Education and Language

The students who feel the safest, the most comfortable, and the most enthused are those who received some form of cultural education in school. Whether cultural studies are a validation of the cultural lives of the students or whether they engender pride and interest in community, they seem to foster individual empowerment. Schools that are highly sensitive to the cultural makeup of their students and promote appropriate multicultural education as fundamental to learning provide the best contexts for both learning and mentorship. Furthermore, language training is fundamental to personal empowerment through cultural education. The students in our research express a rather consistent sentiment that traditional languages should be given credence at least equal to the two charter languages in Canada. We concur with this position: Aboriginal language training should be a fundamental part of a mainstream school curriculum in Saskatchewan schools and in other schools throughout Canada where numbers warrant the inclusion of such training. The findings demonstrate, as well, that it is important for Aboriginal children in mainstream and alternative schools to have access to Elders for cultural and personal training. Students often express the importance of Elders in helping them get and maintain a sense of balance inside and outside of school, and we contend that training by Elders will greatly enhance both the formal and informal acquisition of education.

Recommendation 4: Social and Economic Sensitivity

Students' sensitivity to the problems of poverty, abuse, violence, and parenting illustrates how profoundly socio-economic problems affect the emotional as well as the physical lives of students. The students in our research indicate amazingly high levels of educational aspirations. The likelihood of reaching those aspirations is based, in part, on experiences outside school. For many students in our research, the balance between success and failure is delicate. Schools need to address the familial and community exigencies of the students in the programming and services they offer. This is a difficult task. A responsive education policy, nonetheless, must involve tolerance and understanding for individual misconduct that results from life circumstances, and must demonstrate schools' commitment to rectify damaging conditions. Several alternative high schools and community schools, for example, have cost-recovery breakfast and lunch programs that meet the imme-diate needs of the students and parents. The students and parents con-tribute funds for the program if they are able to and, generally, enough funds are generated by parents and the community to sustain the pro-gram. In addition, two alternative schools in our study incorporate par-enthood training and drug abuse counselling as part of the life skills program. These programs, while somewhat specific to certain popula-tions, indicate that the lived experiences of students can be incorporat-ed into a holistic learning context.

Recommendation 5: Teacher Quality

Good teachers dramatically enhance the enthusiasm of students for learning and poor teachers dramatically damage that enthusiasm. Our concern is that the damage that an insensitive and intolerant teacher does outweighs the benefits that most good teachers generate. It is our firm belief that schools and school boards—especially in Aboriginal communities but not exclusive to such communities—must take care to foster positive teaching, especially among those teachers who are indif-ferent or cynical. Since students (and often their teachers) know full well the teachers who create a negative atmosphere, their input should be sought in discussions of staffing needs. Admittedly, this is a sensitive and complex issue. However, since our research has uncovered the damage that one indifferent or aggressive teacher can do, we feel compelled to offer this as an integral education and human rights issue. Many of the students we interviewed described encounters, usually with only one or two teachers, that left them feeling badly about themselves and about school in general.

In this regard, it should be stressed that while cultural sensitivity is fundamental to positive teaching, being of Aboriginal ancestry is not a necessary condition for cultural sensitivity.

Recommendation 6: Educational Aspirations

Our research finds that both elementary and high school students indi-cate an overwhelming desire to attend some post-secondary education-al institution, especially university. We are also aware that such high aspirations often do not translate into reality, especially for Aboriginal students from northern communities. It would therefore seem incumbent that all schools, but especially isolated rural and northern schools, focus on helping students understand the reality of post-secondary education by offering, on an ongoing basis, information on funding potential; the educational requirements of post-secondary institutions, including programs for Aboriginal students; the social reality of university and college life for Aboriginal students; and the reality of moving from rural to urban areas.

Finally, our research argues for a longer-term initiative regarding long-distance post-secondary education. We maintain that the high aspirations of the students would be fostered by some mechanism of decentralized learning that would provide education to the more isolated areas in Saskatchewan and other provinces and territories. Typical examples include the University of Saskatchewan Northern Teacher Education Program (NORTEP) based in La Ronge in northern Saskatchewan, and the Akitsiraq law school in Iqaluit, Nunavut, which is accredited through the University of Victoria. As it stands, post-secondary education occurs in largely urban contexts and rural and northern students are disadvantaged as a result. For distance education policy, like all of the policy recommendations derived from our research, we reiterate the by now familiar refrain that Aboriginal communities must be fully involved in all aspects of educational decision-making and schooling practice.

THE FUTURE

We advocate for an education system that situates itself at the heart of all forms of advocacy for children, that teaches children the value of their voices by respecting those voices rather than attempting to silence them. We contend that schools have a pivotal role in social justice for youth. Only part of their role is intellectual development. They are arenas of justice, personal development, collective action, and individual achievement. They are also, in many cases, safe houses. The policies that we discuss include making children's lives better by providing a context of (1) emotional and physical safety; (2) achievable day-to-day tasks; (3) democratic education; (4) forums for personal and collective justice; and (5) a comfortable physical environment. We argue that such ideals can be accomplished by bringing the community in, by providing life education, by extending education beyond the 9:00 to 3:30 time frame, and by combining justice and education. We are convinced that what we learn about making such an education better for the increasing numbers of children declared to be at risk is essential to making schools and society better for all children.

The initial chapters in this book document how education was a large component of the historical and structural forces that oppressed Aboriginal people in Canada. For First Nations Canadians, formal education was rarely a force for personal, social, or economic enhancement. It was, in effect, a force for genocide. What we illustrate in this book is that a paradigm shift in education can dramatically alter and redress the historical and contemporary damage experienced by Aboriginal people in Canada, and that small parts of such a fundamental shift are occurring in both rural and urban Aboriginal communities.

QUESTIONS FOR CRITICAL THOUGHT

1. Do alternative education models represent a new way of thinking about and conceptualizing education or are they only minor adjustments to the existing system of conventional education?
2. Summarize the democratic principles that frame the models of education discussed in this book.
3. Discuss the proposition that educational models and policies directed towards helping the most marginalized children and youth would be effective models of learning for all students.
4. It can be argued that education is mostly about social justice and that models of education must reflect issues of equality, caring, community, etc. Discuss this position.
5. Is it a reasonable expectation that schools should be fiscally responsible? Discuss this position with respect to education as a major part of public spending.

RECOMMENDED READING

Haig-Brown, Celia, Jo-Ann Archibald, Robert Regnier, and Kathy Vermette. 1997. *Making the Spirit Dance Within: Joe Duquette High School and an Aboriginal Community.* Toronto: Lorimer.

   The authors present a striking case study, completed in conjunction with Aboriginal students and community members, of a Saskatoon high school that has adopted Aboriginal spirituality, including the sacred circle, as its guiding principle. They examine the school's philosophy, curriculum, and

core programs and activities. The book, like the school, incorporates the viewpoints of students, staff, parents, Elders, and community members.
Ryan, Joan. 1995. *Doing Things the Right Way: Dene Traditional Justice in Lac La Martre, N.W.T.* Calgary: University of Calgary Press.
Through her discussions with Dene Elders, Ryan illustrates the importance of Dogrib traditional justice as the people of Lac La Martre, NWT, struggle to create an atmosphere of community justice that incorporates all elements of existence, including education and mentoring.

PROTOCOL AND RESEARCHER EXPERIENCES AND REFLECTIONS

To fulfill the expectations of this research project, requests were sent out to the Saskatchewan Board of Education, Saskatoon Catholic Board of Education, the Northern Lights School Division, Prince Albert School Division, Qu'Appelle School Division, and the North Battleford School Division. Following is an overview of the researchers' impression of the schools in which interviews and talking circles were conducted.

ELEMENTARY SCHOOL I

This was the first school contacted in the research project. It was chosen for comparative purposes because of its low ratio of Aboriginal students. The principal was very co-operative and interested in this research project. The first meeting with the principal involved reviewing the intent of the research project, the students to be targeted, and how best to conduct the interviews. The principal was open to suggestions from the researchers as to how to access the students to be interviewed.

Within a week, arrangements were made for the students to be interviewed. The teachers from grade 3 and 6 classrooms were notified and the students were called from their classrooms. After each student was interviewed he/she returned to the classroom and sent the next student. The principal provided a vacant room for the interviews. Both the teachers and the principal were very co-operative in assisting with the research project.

ELEMENTARY SCHOOL II

The principal was accommodating by allowing the researchers to take the initiative as to how to proceed with conducting the interviews. After a discussion of the intent of the research project and the students to be targeted, the principal provided two rooms/areas for the interviews to be conducted in and left the interviewing process in the hands of the researchers. Each student was called by the researchers and walked back to his/her class. The basic feeling received from the students after the interviews was that they did not understand what the research was about (i.e., what 'community' was, how they fit into it, or the difference between them and the general population).

The teachers themselves were friendly and open to discussion with the researchers during lunch hour and coffee breaks. It is felt that the ease of entering this school is a result of Tina Nicotine's prior knowledge and contact with the principal. We had intended to interview students from the Adult Learning Centre at this school, but at that time they were preparing for GED exams.

ELEMENTARY SCHOOL III

The principal welcomed the researchers and provided a tour of the school, as well as introductions to the teachers whose students would be interviewed. During the tour and discussion of the research project, the principal made a comment to one of the classrooms that the reason for this research must be that the Board of Education has some extra money.

The scheduled day for the interviews happened to be the school's 'Cultural Awareness Day'. The students participated in various activities that had an Aboriginal component to them (i.e., storytellers, crafts, and talking circles). The person scheduled to conduct the talking circles was not able to make it, and the school asked if the researchers would fulfill this component. We agreed to do this in the morning and start interviews in the afternoon. The cultural awareness activities were scheduled for the morning and recreational activities were scheduled for some grades in the afternoon.

HIGH SCHOOL I

The principal was very excited about the research project itself and was willing to discuss the numerous changes that the school had made regarding the all-encompassing approach to the various needs of the students. Arrangements were made to discuss the project and the process with an Elder who was the 'Stay-in-School' co-ordinator.

The Elder provided names of the students she felt would be interested in participating in the research project. In scheduling the interviews, the Elder was open and accommodating to the schedule of both the students and researcher. A room for conducting the interviews was provided by the school. A list of students was given to the school secretary, who called them in turn to the office where they were met by the researcher. Upon completion of each interview, the student walked back to the main hallway.

HIGH SCHOOL II

Immediately upon entering this school, we could sense a relaxed and informal atmosphere. Both students and teachers were receptive, listening intently to what was being said. If they did not understand, they would ask for clarification. Even though there were a couple of students who were very vocal, each student was given the opportunity either to pass or to talk during the talking circle. Each student spoke to the researchers and provided important information and ideas as to what does and does not work in the mainstream school setting.

After the talking circle, the researchers were invited to stay for lunch. Students and teachers discussed general issues with the researchers on a more informal basis. It was found to be a time to test the researchers in their life situations (i.e., testing one of the researchers on her ability to speak Cree). The principal expressed his belief that the large size of classrooms in mainstream schools does not allow for the closeness or individuality of the students to be considered.

HIGH SCHOOL III

The principal welcomed the researchers and discussed with them the best approach for accessing students. She talked with the students and introduced the researcher to them. A room was set up and each student was asked if he/she minded being tape-recorded. They were also informed that participation was strictly voluntary. All students participated in the interviews.

All of the students had voluntarily enrolled in the school. Many not only attended school, but had families and jobs as well. The students were both open in their discussion and inquisitive about the project.

APPENDIX B

INTERVIEW GUIDE

THEMES

1. Identity

Who is Aboriginal in your family?
Father
Mother
Grandparents on Father's side
Grandparents on Mother's side

Are you:
Métis?
First Nation? If yes, which one?
Non-Status?
Inuk?

2. Language

Does anyone in your home speak an Aboriginal language? If yes,
which one?
Do you speak an Aboriginal language?
What Aboriginal language do you speak and/or understand?
Can you write an Aboriginal language?
Who taught you to speak an Aboriginal language?

3. School

What do you like about school?
What is difficult about school?
Are there Aboriginal teachers in your school?
What are you taught about Aboriginal culture?
Do you want to continue with school?

Do you want to go to school at a technical college, university, trade school?

What do you not like about your school, i.e., other teachers, students, etc.?

What do you think are some barriers to learning?

poverty conditions
unemployment
housing
abuse-related issues
difficulty in learning—do not like to be in school
racism
schools do not teach about Aboriginal culture
teachers are not open to talking to you

4. Social issues

What do you think are some problems for Aboriginal people in your community?

suicide
unemployment
housing
family violence
abuse issues
addictions
racism
youth recreation
programming
daycare
not enough to do

5. Work-related activities

What do your parents do for a living?

What types of work do people do in your community—hunting, trapping, crafts, business, school, band office, health worker, counsellor, Chief, government, social worker?

What kind of job would you like to have in the future?

WEB SITES

http://www.aboriginalcanada.com/firstnation

This Web site provides a directory of Aboriginal Nations in Canada in order to increase the availability of contact information for Aboriginal communities. The site is organized by province and territory. The voluntary nature of the site means that only those First Nations who posted contact information are included.

http://www.aboriginalrightscoalition.ca

The Aboriginal Rights Coalition includes churches working in partnership with Aboriginal peoples and their communities. One aim of the ARC is to act as an advocacy group for Aboriginal issues, such as in working towards the recognition of land rights. In addition, the ARC discusses the importance of reversing the erosion of Aboriginal peoples' social rights in Canada. Finally, language and education are purported to be central to the mission of the ARC. The ARC was conceived in 1975 and, thus, provides primarily current but some historical information on Aboriginal land claims and rights struggles in Canada.

http://www.afn.ca

The Assembly of First Nations Web site includes program listings for Aboriginal people, press releases about current issues affecting the lives of Aboriginal people in Canada, and current events in the Canadian Aboriginal community. Major areas of concern such as education, health, housing, land rights, and language are addressed here. The site includes the formal policies and objectives of the Assembly of First Nations and the formal stand of the Assembly on current events, such as the Burnt Church fishing dispute. This site is a useful source for information on current news events and the position of the representatives of Aboriginal communities in Canada.

http://www.ainc-inac.gc.ca

Indian and Northern Affairs is a department of the federal government of Canada. Indian and Northern Affairs offers information on the programs and services it offers, as well as on culture and history. The site also contains research resources and publications, including statistics on education and First Nations. Further, the department has posted a copy of the Report of the Royal Commission on Aboriginal Peoples in addition to other significant agreements, such as rights claims and treaties.

http://www.Anglican.ca/ministry/rs/reports

This is the official Web site of the Anglican Church of Canada on the residential school legacy and the Anglican Church's response. The site includes reports and news releases dealing with the Anglican Church and its role in the operation of residential schools as well as current developments on the issue. The Anglican Church uses this site to make a formal apology to Aboriginal people in Canada and outlines its aims towards healing and reconciliation. The site also contains information on residential schools, litigation, and alternative dispute resolution processes.

http://www.asa.nsw.edu.au/journals.html

The Aboriginal Studies Association lists information on its *Journal of the Aboriginal Studies*. The journal includes articles relevant to Aboriginal education techniques and provides both an academic and a non-academic forum for the discussion of Aboriginal studies. The site also contains a list of resources and information about conferences on Aboriginal studies.

http://www.athabascau.ca/indigenous

This site primarily contains information on the indigenous education program at Athabasca University, including contact information for staff and faculty. However, it also includes research resources through its library home page, such as databases, Inuit resources, global indigenous resources, and the university archives. In addition, the site contains links relevant to First Nations, Métis, and Inuit education, language, and law and governance. This site is an excellent resource for research on indigenous education.

http://www.aybc.org/resource/content/faay.htm

The Canadian Council for Aboriginal Business created the Foundation for the Advancement of Aboriginal Youth. The Foundation receives money from corporate donors such as the Bank of Montreal to support Aboriginal youth bursary and scholarship programs. The site provides contact information for Aboriginal youth interested in applying for the scholarship and bursary programs. The Foundation is also engaged in other initiatives, including conferences, speakers, resource groups, and the publication of the *Canadian Aboriginal Journal*.

http://www.ayn.ca/

The Aboriginal Youth Network Web site is a space for Aboriginal youth to meet, chat, and access resources relevant to their culture and communities. The site primarily contains news articles, information on current events, and contests. Links to education and employment resources and an e-mail service are provided for Aboriginal youth. The site can be compared to a community centre because of the resources it offers and the space it provides for Aboriginal youth to meet and discuss issues relevant to their lives.

http://www.bced.gov.bc.ca/abed

The British Columbia Ministry of Education outlines on this site its policies on Aboriginal education and its commitment to increasing the success of Aboriginal students. This site offers an example of provincial and territorial policy surrounding Aboriginal education initiatives. The site also includes a list of links relevant to Aboriginal education in Canada.

http://www.Bloorstreet.com/300block/aborl.htm

This site has links to Aboriginal resources in a variety of countries, including Canada, America, Australia, and New Zealand. Some categories are cultural, environmental, human rights issues, Aboriginal arts, Aboriginal law, and legislation affecting Aboriginals that is available on-line. The site also includes a large number of links to treaties under the country categories. Bill Henderson, a Toronto lawyer, created this site.

http://www.brandonu.ca/Organizations/EAGLES/

Elders and Graduate Level Educators is partially funded by Canadian Heritage through Brandon University. The organization draws together Elders and Aboriginal scholars in order to preserve indigenous knowledge and contributes to current research projects through the dissemination of indigenous knowledge and research pertaining to Aboriginal peoples.

http://canada.justice.gc.ca

The Department of Justice Canada site lists programs and services offered by the Justice Department, including those developed for Aboriginal people. The Aboriginal Justice portion of the site includes the Aboriginal Justice Learning Network, a broad-based volunteer organization of representatives from the conventional justice system and Aboriginal communities. The Justice Department established the Aboriginal Justice Learning Network in 1996.

http://www.canadianaboriginal.com

The Canadian Aboriginal Web site offers a wide range of news and current event articles relevant to the Aboriginal community in Canada.The site also offers articles on legal, political, education, criminal, and Aboriginal activism, and provides links to other Aboriginal magazines and on-line resources. The site is a good source for investigating current issues relevant to First Nations in Canada.

http://www.ceso-saco.com/aboriginalsvc.htm

This site is operated by the Canadian Executive Services Organization, a group that provides volunteer business advisers to Aboriginal peoples. The organization's goals are to increase the self-sufficiency and self-determination of Aboriginal people.

http://www.citytel.net/rcmp/nirstf.htm

This site provides information on the Native Residential School Task

Force and its mandate. The site includes a description of the Task Force, the scope of its investigation, victim support information, and contact information.

http://www.cwis.org
The Centre for World Indigenous Studies seeks to democratize relations between peoples, nations, and states in a manner based on co-operation rather than conflict. The CWIS Web site strives to offer a world perspective on indigenous studies and accounts of the relationships between peoples and nations through facilitating the transfer of experience and ideas. The site includes a list of resources and programs delivered through the organization, as well as information on the organization internship and fellowship programs.

http://www.Indigenous.bc.ca
The Institute of Indigenous Government in British Columbia offers courses in post-secondary learning. The Institute is an example of Aboriginal education or alternative education programs for Aboriginal people in Canada.

http://www.inorth.on.ca/~giboskab/
This site is a resource for survivors of residential schools and contains first-person accounts of the residential school system. The purpose of the site is to extend support to the survivors by providing information on the issue through direct communication between the survivors themselves.

http://library.usask.ca/native
The University of Saskatchewan Library offers a variety of resources for Aboriginal Studies and in particular studies in Aboriginal education. The library offers photos, archival material, Native law cases, electronic journals, etc. Access to the catalogue and many other resources is open to everyone; however, some resources are restricted to university students, staff, and faculty.

http://juliet.stfx.ca/people/fac/rmackinn/native.htm
This site has both Canadian and American Aboriginal links, though the links are not divided into further sub-categories. The links include information relevant to Aboriginal education and educators. The site was created by Fred Pashe and is housed at St Francis Xavier University.

http://www.Nativeweb.org/resources
This site includes resources for indigenous cultures around the world. Categories include libraries, Elders, organizations, business and economy, education, information (different forms of news such as newspapers), and environment.

http://www.oise.utoronto.ca/~first/
The Aboriginal Education Resource Database is housed by the Indigenous Education Network at the Ontario Institute for Studies in Education at the

University of Toronto. The database primarily focuses on post-secondary education at Canadian institutions and is a useful tool for finding information on Aboriginal education and post-secondary institutions in Canada.

http://www.oise.utoronto.ca/other/ien/ienpage.html

The Indigenous Education Network is a self-determining organization founded in 1989 by Aboriginal students and who now provide an Aboriginal presence at OISE/University of Toronto. The Indigenous Education Network operates in collaboration with the Aboriginal Students' Caucus at the Ontario Institute for Studies in Education. The Indigenous Education Network, among other tasks, provides support for students interested in the study of Aboriginal education, promotes Aboriginal education, advances research on Aboriginal education issues, and supports Aboriginal education curriculum development. The site includes a description of programs, scholarships, and links to other sites of interest to Aboriginal and indigenous education.

http://www.ptla.org/wabanaki/Webshu.htm

The Wabanaki Legal News site contains an article written by Patricia Doyle Bedwell on 'Compensation for Residential School Survivors'. Patricia Bedwell is the head of the Transition Year Program at Hension College in Halifax, Nova Scotia. The article provides the author's professional account and analysis of the issue.

http://www.sdc.uwo.ca/firstN

First Nations Services of the University of Western Ontario is mandated in the areas of recruitment and advancement of First Nations peoples as students and employees. In addition, it offers culturally supportive services to First Nations students attending the University of Western Ontario.

http://www.treaty7org/document/circle/circlint.htm

The Circle Game: Shadows and Substance in the Indian Residential School Experience in Canada is a report that was submitted to the Royal Commission on Aboriginal peoples in October 1994 by Roland D. Chrisjohn and Sherri L. Young with contributions by Michael Maraun. The report has been published as a book but is posted for use on this Web site. The text contains a review of Aboriginal peoples and the residential school system in Canada.

http://www.usask.ca/nativelaw

The Native Law Centre of Canada offers a directory of publications, news, and residential schools information. Court decisions surrounding residential schools are featured in addition to other legal cases relevant to Aboriginal people and the Canadian legal system.

BIBLIOGRAPHY

Adams, Howard. 1990. *Prison of Grass*, 2nd edn. Saskatoon: Fifth House Publishers.

Alladin, Ibrahim. 1996. *Racism in Canadian Schools*. Toronto: Harcourt Brace and Company.

Anderson, Robert Brent. 1999. *Economic Development among the Aboriginal Peoples in Canada: The Hope for the Future*. North York, Ont.: Captus Press.

Angus, Murray. 1991. *'And the Last Shall Be First': Native Policy in an Era of Cutbacks*. Toronto: NC Press.

Archibald, Jo-Ann. 1995. 'To Keep the Fire Going: The Challenge for First Nations Education in the Year 2000', in Ratna Ghosh and Douglas Ray, eds, *Social Change and Education in Canada*, 3rd edn. Toronto: Harcourt Brace & Company, 342–57.

———— and Celia Haig-Brown. 1995. *The Exemplary Schools Project: Peguis Central School*. Toronto: Canadian Education Association.

Armstrong, R., J. Kennedy, and P.R. Oberle. 1990. *University Education and Economic Well-Being: Indian Achievement and Prospects*. Ottawa: Indian and Northern Affairs Canada.

Assembly of First Nations. 1994. *Breaking the Chains: First Nations Literacy and Self-Determination*. Ottawa: Assembly of First Nations.

Barman, Jean, Yvonne Hébert, and Don McCaskill. 1986. 'The Legacy of the Past: An Overview', in Barman, Hébert, and McCaskill, eds, *Indian Education in Canada: Volume 1: The Legacy*. Vancouver: University of British Columbia Press, 1–22.

Battiste, Marie, ed. 2000. *Reclaiming Indigenous Voice and Vision*. Vancouver: University of British Columbia Press.

———— and Jean Barman, eds. 1995. *First Nations Education in Canada: The Circle Unfolds*. Vancouver: University of British Columbia Press.

———— and James (Sa'ke'j) Henderson. 2000. *Protecting Indigenous Knowledge and Heritage: A Global Challenge*. Saskatoon: Purich Publishing.

Berger, Thomas. 1991. *A Long and Terrible Shadow: White Values, Natives Rights in the Americas, 1492–1992*. Vancouver: Douglas & McIntyre.

Bernier, Rachel. 1997. *The Dimensions of Wage Inequality among Aboriginal Peoples*. Ottawa: Statistics Canada, Analytical Studies Branch Research Paper Series No. 109, Dec.

Boldt, Menno. 1993. *Surviving as Indians: The Challenge of Self-Government*. Toronto: University of Toronto Press.

Brady, Patrick. 1991. 'An Analysis of Program Delivery Services in First Nations, Federal, and Provincial Schools in Northwestern Ontario', *Canadian Journal of Native Education* 18, 1: 65–72.

———. 1992. 'Individual or Group Representation: Native Trustees on Boards of Education in Ontario', *Canadian Journal of Native Education* 19, 1: 67–72.

Burns, George. 1998. 'Factors and Themes in Native Education and School Boards/First Nations Tuition Negotiations and Tuition Agreement Schooling', *Canadian Journal of Native Education* 22, 1: 53–66.

Cairns, Alan C. 2000. *Citizens Plus: Aboriginal Peoples and the Canadian State*. Vancouver: University of British Columbia Press.

Cajete, Gregory. 1999. *Ignite the Sparkle: An Indigenous Science Model*. Skyland, NC: Kivaki Press.

Campbell, Mary I. 1991. 'Teachers' Perceptions of Learning Styles and Teaching Strategies in Relation to Children of Indian Ancestry', M.Ed. thesis, University of Regina.

Canadian Council on Social Development. 2000. *Unequal Access: A Canadian Profile of Racial Differences in Education, Employment and Income*. A Report Prepared for Canadian Race Relations Foundation. Toronto: Canadian Race Relations Foundation.

Canadian Labour Force Development Board. 1994. *Putting the Pieces Together: Toward a Coherent Transition System for Canada's Labour Force*. Report of the Task Force on Transition into Employment. Ottawa: Canadian Labour Force Development Board.

Cardinal, Harold. 1977. *The Rebirth of Canada's Indians*. Edmonton: Hurtig.

Carrigan, D. Owen. 1998. *Juvenile Delinquency in Canada: A History*. Concord, Ont.: Irwin Publishing.

Castellano, Marlene Brant, Lynne Davis, and Louise Lahache, eds. 2000a. *Aboriginal Education: Fulfilling the Promise*. Vancouver: University of British Columbia Press.

———, ———, and ———. 2000b. 'Conclusion: Fulfilling the Promise', in Castellano et al. (2000a: 251–5).

Chisholm, Shirley. 1994. 'Assimilation and Oppression: The Northern Experience', *Education Canada* 34, 4 (Winter): 28–34.

Chrisjohn, Roland, and Sherri Young. 1997. *The Circle Game: Shadows and Substance in the Indian Residential School Experience in Canada*. Penticton, BC: Theytus Books.

Coleman, Michael C. 1993. *American Indian Children at School, 1850–1930*.

Jackson: University Press of Mississippi.

Common, Ron. 1991. 'A search for equity: A policy analysis of First Nations representation on school boards', *Education Canada* 31, 3 (Fall): 4–7.

Cote, Helen. 2001. 'Damaged Children and Broken Spirits: An Examination of Attitudes of Anisnabek Elders to Acts of Violence amongst Anisnabek Youth', MA thesis University of Saskatchewan.

Council of Ministers of Education Canada. 1996. *Enhancing the Role of Teachers in a Changing World*. Toronto: Council of Ministers of Education Canada.

Cummins, Jim. 1986. 'Empowering Minority Students: A Framework for Intervention', *Harvard Educational Review* 56, 1 (Feb.): 18–36.

de Brouker, Patrice, and Laval Lavallée. 1998. 'Getting ahead in life: Does your parents' education count?', *Education Quarterly Review* 5, 1 (Aug.): 22–8. Statistics Canada Catalogue no. 81–003-XPB.

Deiter, Constance. 1998. *From Our Mothers' Arms: The Intergenerational Impact of Residential Schools in Saskatchewan*. Toronto: United Church Publishing House.

Department of Indian Affairs and Northern Development Canada (DIAND). 1997. *Socio-Economic Indicators in Indian Reserves and Comparable Communities 1971–1991*. Ottawa: Minister of Public Works and Government Services Canada.

———. 1998. *Basic Departmental Data 1997*. Ottawa: Minister of Public Works and Government Services Canada.

———. 2000. *Basic Departmental Data 1999*. Ottawa: Minister of Public Works and Government Services Canada.

Deyhle, Donna. 1986. 'Success and Failure: A Micro-Ethnographic Comparison of Navajo and Anglo Students' Perceptions of Testing', *Curriculum Inquiry* 16, 4 (Winter): 365–89.

——— and Karen Swisher. 1997. 'Research in American Indian and Alaska Native Education: From Assimilation to Self-Determination', in Michael W. Apple, ed., *Review of Research in Education*, vol. 22. Washington: American Educational Research Association, 113–94.

Dickason, Olive Patricia. 2001. *Canada's First Nations: A History of Founding Peoples from Earliest Times*, 3rd edn. Toronto: Oxford University Press.

Douglas, Anne S. 1994. 'Recontextualizing Schooling Within an Inuit Community', *Canadian Journal of Education* 19, 2: 154–64.

Druian, Greg, and Jocelyn A. Butler. 1997. 'Effective Schooling Practices and At-Risk Youth: What the Research Shows'. Portland, Ore.: Northwest Regional Educational Laboratory, School Improvement Research Series, Topical Synthesis #1.

Dunn, K., and C. Runyan. 1993. 'Deaths at Work Among Children and Adolescents', *American Journal of Diseases in Children* 147: 1044–7.

Emberley, Julia. 1996. 'Aboriginal Women's Writing and the Cultural Politics of Representation', in C. Miller and P. Chuchryk, eds, *Women of the First Nations: Power, Wisdom, and Strength*. Winnipeg: University of Manitoba Press, 97–112.

Federation of Saskatchewan Indian Nations. 1997. *Saskatchewan and Aboriginal Peoples in the 21st Century: Social, Economic and Political Changes and Challenges*. Regina: PrintWest Publishing.

Fettes, Mark, and Ruth Norton. 2000. 'Voices of Winter: Aboriginal Languages and Public Policy in Canada', in Castellano et al. (2000a: 29–54).

Fine, Michelle. 1993. 'Making Controversy: Who's "At-Risk"?', in Roberta Woloons, ed., *Children at Risk in America: History, Concepts, and Public Policy*. Albany: State University of New York Press, 91–110.

Fiske, Jo-Anne. 1996. 'Gender and the Paradox of Residential Education in Carrier Society', in Christine Miller and Patricia Chuchryk, eds, *Women of the First Nations: Power, Wisdom, and Strength*. Winnipeg: University of Manitoba Press, 167–82.

Flanagan, Thomas. 2000. *First Nations? Second Thoughts*. Montreal: McGill-Queen's University Press.

Fleras, Augie, and Jean Leonard Elliott. 1996. *Unequal Relations: An Introduction to Race, Ethnic and Aboriginal Dynamics in Canada*, 2nd edn. Scarborough, Ont.: Prentice-Hall.

——— and Paul Spoonley. 1999. *Recalling Aotearoa: Indigenous Politics and Ethnic Relations in New Zealand*. Auckland, NZ: Oxford University Press.

Frideres, James S. 1998. *Aboriginal Peoples in Canada: Contemporary Conflicts*, 5th edn. Scarborough, Ont.: Prentice-Hall Allyn and Bacon Canada.

Foot, David K., with Daniel Stoffman. 1996. *Boom, Bust and Echo: How to Profit from the Coming Demographic Shift*. Toronto: Macfarlane Walter and Ross.

Furniss, Elizabeth. 1999. *The Burden of History: Colonialism and the Frontier Myth in a Rural Canadian Community*. Vancouver: University of British Columbia Press.

Gabriel Dumont Institute of Native Studies and Applied Research. 1993. *Saskatchewan Métis Family Literacy and Youth Education Strategy: A Provincial Strategy*, submitted to the Royal Commission on Aboriginal Peoples, Sept. Saskatoon: Gabriel Dumont Institute of Native Studies and Applied Research.

Gaskell, Jane. 1995. *Secondary Schools in Canada: The National Report of the Exemplary Schools Project*. Toronto: Canadian Education Association.

Gatto, John Taylor. 1992. *Dumbing Us Down: The Hidden Curriculum of*

Compulsory Schooling. Gabriola Island, BC: New Society Publishers.

Gilbert, Sid, Lynn Barr, Warren Clark, Matthew Blue, and Deborah Sunter. 1993. *Leaving School: Results from a National Survey*. Ottawa: Minister of Supply and Services Canada.

————— and Jeff Frank. 1998. 'Educational Pathways', in Human Resources Development Canada, *High School May Not Be Enough: An Analysis of Results from the School Leavers Follow-up Survey, 1995*. Ottawa: Minister of Public Works and Government Services Canada, 9–20.

Government of Canada. 1999. *Background: Balancing Choices: Opportunities in Science and Technology for Aboriginal People*. Ottawa: Minister of Public Works and Government Services Canada.

Graveline, Fyre Jean. 1998. *Circle Works: Transforming Eurocentric Consciousness*. Halifax: Fernwood Publishing.

Gregory, Lynn W. 1995. 'The "Turnaround" Process: Factors Influencing the School Success of Urban Youth', *Journal of Adolescent Research* 10, 1 (Jan.): 136–54.

Guppy, Neil, and Scott Davies. 1998. *Education in Canada: Recent Trends and Future Challenges*. Ottawa: Statistics Canada, Catalogue no. 96–321-MPE No. 3.

Guy, Kathleen, ed. 1997. *Our Promise to Children*. Ottawa: Canadian Institute of Child Health.

Haig-Brown, Celia. 1988. *Resistance and Renewal: Surviving the Indian Residential School*. Vancouver: Tillacum Library.

—————, Jo-Ann Archibald, Robert Regnier, and Kathy Vermette. 1997. *Making the Spirit Dance Within: Joe Duquette High School and an Aboriginal Community*. Lorimer.

Hamilton, A.C., and Murray Sinclair. 1991. *Report of the Aboriginal Justice Inquiry of Manitoba*. Winnipeg: Queen's Printer.

Hamilton, W.D. 1991. *Closing the Gap: The Native Indian Students' Achievement Study*. Fredericton: Department of Education, Province of New Brunswick.

Hampton, Eber, and Steven Wolfson. 1994 'Education for Self-Determination', in John H. Hylton, ed., *Aboriginal Self-Government in Canada: Current Trends and Issues*. Saskatoon: Purich Publishing, 90–8.

Hawthorn, H.B. 1967. *A Survey of the Contemporary Indians of Canada: Economic, Political, and Educational Needs*. Ottawa: Indian Affairs Branch.

Hébert, Yvonne. 2000. 'The State of Aboriginal Literacy and Language Education', in Castellano et al. (2000a: 55–75).

Hern, Matt. 1996. *Deschooling Our Lives*. Gabriola Island, BC: New Society Publishers.

Herrnstein, Richard J., and Charles Murray. 1994. *The Bell Curve: Intelligence and*

Class Structure in American Life. New York: The Free Press.

Hesch, Rick. 1995. 'Aboriginal Teachers as Organic Intellectuals', in Roxana Ng, Pat Staton, and Joyce Scane, eds, *Anti-Racism, Feminism, and Critical Approaches to Education.* Toronto: OISE Press, 99–128.

Hess, Melanie. 1989. *Children, Schools and Poverty.* Ottawa: Canadian Teachers' Federation.

Hull, Jeremy. 2000. *Aboriginal Post-Secondary Education and Labour Market Outcomes, Canada, 1996.* Ottawa: Department of Indian Affairs and Northern Development.

Human Resources Development Canada. 2000. *Job Futures 2000.* Ottawa.

Hylton, John H., ed. 1999a. *Aboriginal Self-Government in Canada: Current Trends and Issues,* 2nd edn. Saskatoon: Purich Publishing.

————. 1999b. 'The Case for Self-Government: A Social Policy Perspective', in Hylton (1999a: 78–91).

Jaine, Linda, ed. 1993. *Residential Schools: The Stolen Years.* Saskatoon: University Extension Press, University of Saskatchewan.

Jankowski, W.B., and B. Moazzami. 1995. 'Returns of Education Among Northwestern Ontario's Native People', *Canadian Journal of Native Studies* 15, 1: 103–11.

Jenkins, Jenny, and Daniel Keating. 1998. *Risk and Resilience in Six- and Ten-Year-Old Children.* Ottawa: Human Resources Development Canada, Applied Research Branch Strategy Policy W-98–23E.

Jenness, Diamond. 1977. *The Indians of Canada,* 7th edn. Toronto: University of Toronto Press.

Kachur, Jerrold L. 1999. 'Quasi-Marketing Education: The Entrepreneurial State and Charter Schooling in Alberta', in Dave Broad and Wayne Antony, eds, *Citizens or Consumers? Social Policy in a Market Society.* Halifax: Fernwood Publishing, 129–50.

Kehoe, Jack, and Frank Echols. 1994. 'Improving Achievement and Other Outcomes Among Urban Native Students', *Canadian Journal of Native Studies* 14, 1: 61–75.

Kincheloe, Joe, ed. 1998. *White Reign: Deploying Whiteness in America.* New York: St Martin's Press.

King, Alan J.C., and Marjorie J. Peart. 1992. *Teachers in Canada: Their Work and Quality of Life.* Ottawa: Canadian Teachers' Federation.

Kirkness, Verna, and Sheena Selkirk Bowman. 1992. *First Nations and Schools: Triumphs and Struggles.* Toronto: Canadian Education Association.

Knockwood, Isabelle. 1992. *Out of the Depths: The Experiences of Mi'kmaw Children at the Indian Residential School at Shubenacadie, Nova Scotia.*

Lockeport, NS: Roseway Publishing.

Kramer, Reinhold, and Tom Mitchell. 2002. *Walk Towards the Gallows: The Tragedy of Hilda Blake, Hanged 1899.* Toronto: Oxford University Press.

Levin, Benjamin, and J. Anthony Riffel. 1997. *Schools and the Changing World: Struggling Towards the Future.* London: The Falmer Press.

Littlejohn, Catherine, and Shirley Fredeen. 1991. 'Indian Language Programs in Saskatchewan: A Survey', in Sonia Morris, Keith McLeod, and Marcel Danesi, eds, *Aboriginal Languages and Education: The Canadian Experience.* Oakville, Ont.: Mosaic Press, 57–81.

Livingstone, D.W. 1999. *The Education-Jobs Gap: Underemployment or Economic Democracy.* Toronto: Garamond Press.

———. 2000. 'Exploring the Icebergs of Adult Learning: Findings of the First Canadian Survey of Informal Learning Practices', New Approaches to Lifelong Learning Working Paper Series 11–2000. Available at: <http://nall.oise.utoronto.ca>.

McDonald, Neil. 1977. 'Canadian Nationalism and North-West Schools, 1884–1905', in Alf Chaiton and Neil McDonald, eds, *Canadian Schools and Canadian Identity.* Toronto: Gage Educational Publishing, 59–87.

McDonnell, R.F., and R.C. Depew. 1999. 'Aboriginal Self-Government and Self-Determination in Canada: A Critical Commentary', in Hylton (1999a: 352–76).

McGinty, Sue. 1999. *Resilience, Gender, and Success at School.* New York: Peter Lang.

McPherson, James C. 1991. *McPherson Report on Tradition and Education: Towards a Vision of Our Future.* Ottawa: Department of Indian Affairs and Northern Development.

Maguire, Mary H., and Lynn McAlpine. 1995. *Attautsikut/Together. Understanding Culture, Change and Success in Qitiqliq Secondary School and Arviat.* Toronto: Canadian Education Association.

Marker, Michael. 2000. 'Economics and Local Self-Determination: Describing the Clash Zone in First Nations Education', *Canadian Journal of Native Education* 24, 1: 30–44.

Melnechenko, Lorri, and Helen Horseman. 1999. 'The Experiences and Attitudes of Aboriginal Teachers in Provincial Schools'. Unpublished research report prepared for Saskatchewan Education, Regina.

Miller, J.R. 1996. *Shingwauk's Vision: A History of Native Residential Schools.* Toronto: University of Toronto Press.

Milloy, John S. 1999. *A National Crime: The Canadian Government and the Residential School System, 1879 to 1986.* Winnipeg: University of Manitoba Press.

Mills Consulting. 1992. *Indian and Métis Education: Present Realities and Future Directions*. Regina: Saskatchewan School Trustees Association Research Centre Report #92–15.

———. 1993. *Indian and Métis Education: Parents as Partners*. Regina: Saskatchewan School Trustees Association Research Centre Report #93–10.

Monture-Angus, Patricia. 1999. *Journeying Forward: Dreaming First Nations' Independence*. Halifax: Fernwood Publishing.

Nagler, Mark. 1975. *Natives without a Home*. Don Mills, Ont.: Longmans.

National Indian Brotherhood/Assembly of First Nations. 1972. *Indian Control of Indian Education: A Position Paper*. Ottawa: National Indian Brotherhood.

———. 1988. *Tradition and Education: Towards a Vision of Our Future*. Territory of Akwesasne, Hamilton's Island, Summerstown, Ont.: National Indian Brotherhood/Assembly of First Nations.

Natriello, Gary, Edward L. McDill, and Aaron M. Pallas. 1990. *Schooling Disadvantaged Children: Racing Against Catastrophe*. New York: Teachers College Press.

Nock, David. 1988. *A Victorian Missionary and Canadian Public Policy: Cultural Synthesis and Cultural Replacement*. Waterloo, Ont.: Wilfrid Laurier University Press.

Norris, Mary Jane. 1998. 'Canada's Aboriginal Languages', *Canadian Social Trends* 51 (Winter): 8–16.

Nuu-chah-nulth Tribal Council. 1996. *Indian Residential Schools: The Nuu-chah-nulth Experience*. Report of the Nuu-chah-nulth Tribal Council Indian Residential School Study, 1992–1994. Port Alberni, BC: Nuu-chah-nulth Tribal Council.

Organization for Economic Co-operation and Development (OECD). 1998. 'Overcoming Failure at School: A Summary of the Draft Report of the OECD', *Education Canada* 38, 2 (Summer): 5–8.

Paquette, Jerald. 1989. 'Policy, Power and Purpose: Lessons from Two Indian Education Scenarios', *Journal of Canadian Studies* 24, 2 (Summer): 78–94.

Parker, D.L. 1997. *Stolen Dreams: Portraits of Working Children*. Minneapolis: Lerner Publications.

Perley, David G. 1992. *Excellence in Education: Improving Aboriginal Education in New Brunswick*. Fredericton: Commission on Excellence in Education.

———. 1993. 'Aboriginal Education in Canada as Internal Colonialism', *Canadian Journal of Native Education* 20, 1: 118–28.

Ponting, J. Rick. 1997. 'Editor's Introduction', in Ponting, ed., *First Nations in Canada: Perspectives on Opportunity, Empowerment, and Self-Determination*. Toronto: McGraw-Hill Ryerson, 3–18.

————. 1998. 'Racism and Stereotyping of First Nations', in Vic Satzewich, ed., *Racism and Social Inequality in Canada: Concepts, Controversies, and Strategies of Resistance*. Toronto: Thompson Educational Publishing, 269–98.

Prentice, Alison. 1977. *The School Promoters: Education and Social Class in Mid-Nineteenth Century Upper Canada*. Toronto: McClelland & Stewart.

Renihan, Frederick, Edward Buller, Wayne Desharnais, Robin Enns, Thérèse Laferrière, and Lorraine Therrien. 1994. *Taking Stock: An Assessment of the National Stay-in-School Initiative*. Ottawa: Human Resources Development Canada.

Research and Analysis Directorate, Department of Indian Affairs and Northern Development. 1999. *Intellectual Property and Aboriginal People: A Working Paper*. Ottawa: Indian and Northern Affairs Canada.

Rice, James J., and Michael J. Prince. 2000. *Changing Politics of Canadian Social Policy*. Toronto: University of Toronto Press.

Richards, John. 2000. 'Reserves Are Only Good for Some People', *Journal of Canadian Studies* 35, 1: 191–202.

Ross, Rupert. 1992. *Dancing with a Ghost: Exploring Indian Reality*. Markham, Ont.: Octopus Publishing.

————. 1996. *Returning to the Teachings: Exploring Aboriginal Justice*. Toronto: Penguin Books.

Royal Commission on Aboriginal Peoples. 1993. *Aboriginal Peoples in Urban Centres: Report of the National Round Table on Aboriginal Urban Issues*. Ottawa: Minister of Supply and Services Canada.

————. 1996a. *Guide to the Principal Findings and Recommendations of the Final Report of the Royal Commission on Aboriginal Peoples*. Ottawa: Minister of Supply and Services Canada.

————. 1996b. *Report of the Royal Commission on Aboriginal Peoples, Volume 1: Looking Forward, Looking Back*. Ottawa: Minister of Supply and Services Canada.

————. 1996c. *Report of the Royal Commission on Aboriginal Peoples, Volume 3: Gathering Strength*. Ottawa: Minister of Supply and Services Canada.

Ryan, James. 1995. 'Experiencing Urban Schooling: The Adjustment of Native Students to the Extra-Curricular Demands of a Post-Secondary Education Program', *Canadian Journal of Native Studies* 15, 2: 211–30.

————. 1996. 'Restructuring First Nations' Education: Trust, Respect and Governance', *Journal of Canadian Studies* 31, 2 (Summer): 115–32.

Ryan, Joan. 1995. *Doing Things the Right Way*. Calgary: University of Calgary Press.

St Denis, Verna. 2002. 'An Exploration of the Socio-Historical Production of

Aboriginal Identity: Implications for Education', doctoral thesis, Stanford University.

———, Rita Bouvier, and Marie Battiste. 1998. 'Okiskinahamakewak—Aboriginal Teachers in Saskatchewan's Publicly Funded Schools: Responding to the Flux'. Unpublished research report prepared for Saskatchewan Education, Regina.

Santiago, Marcia. 1997. *Post-Secondary Education and Labour Market Outcomes for Registered Indians.* Ottawa: Indian Affairs and Northern Development Canada.

Saskatchewan Education. 1985. *The Inner-City Dropout Study.* Regina: Saskatchewan Education.

———. 1991. *Partners in Action: Action Plan of the Indian and Métis Education Advisory Committee.* Regina: Saskatchewan Education.

———. 1996. *Building Communities of Hope: Best Practices for Meeting the Learning Needs of At-Risk and Indian and Métis Students.* Regina: Saskatchewan Education.

Saskatchewan Human Rights Commission. 1999. 'Education Equity, 10-Year Statistical Summary', Statistical Tables produced by Saskatchewan Human Rights Commission.

Saskatchewan Treaty Indians. 1993. *Demographics and Education.* Saskatoon: Office of the Treaty Commissioner.

Satzewich, Vic, and Terry Wotherspoon. 2000. *First Nations: Race, Class and Gender Relations.* Regina: Canadian Plains Research Centre.

Schissel, Bernard. 1993. *The Social Dimensions of Canadian Youth Justice.* Toronto: Oxford University Press.

———. 1997. *Blaming Children: Youth Crime, Moral Panics and the Politics of Hate.* Halifax: Fernwood.

———. 2002. 'The Pathology of Powerlessness: Adolescent Health in Canada', in B. Singh Bolaria and Harley Dickinson, eds, *Health, Illness, and Health Care in Canada.* Toronto: Nelson Thompson, 265–91.

Stairs, Arlene. 1995. 'Learning Processes and Teaching Roles in Native Education: Cultural Base and Cultural Brokerage', in Battiste and Barman (1995: 139–53).

Stamp, Robert M. 1977. 'Canadian Education and National Identity', in Alf Chaiton and Neil McDonald, eds, *Canadian Schools and Canadian Identity.* Toronto: Gage Educational Publishing, 29–37.

Statistics Canada. 1998a. '1996 Census: Aboriginal Data', *The Daily*, 13 Jan.

———. 1998b. '1996 Census: Education, Mobility and Migration', *The Daily*, 14 Apr.

———. 1998c. '1996 Census: Sources of Income, Earnings and Total Income, and Family Income', *The Daily*, 12 May.

———. 1998d. 'Population by Aboriginal Groups and Sex, Showing Age Groups, for Canada, Provinces and Territories, 1996 Census', Statistics Canada Web site: <www.statcan.ca/english/census96/>.

Stevenson, Winona. 1991. 'Prairie Indians and Higher Education: An Historical Overview, 1876 to 1977', in Terry Wotherspoon, ed., *Hitting the Books: The Politics of Educational Retrenchment*. Toronto and Saskatoon: Garamond Press and Social Research Unit, 215–34.

Stout, Cameron W. 1997. 'Nunavut: Canada's Newest Territory in 1999', *Canadian Social Trends* 44 (Spring): 13–18.

Subcommittee on Aboriginal Education. 1996. *Sharing the Knowledge: The Path to Success and Equal Opportunities in Education*. Report of the Standing Committee on Aboriginal Affairs and Northern Development. Ottawa: Canada Communication Group.

Tait, Heather. 1999. 'Educational Achievement of Young Aboriginal Adults', *Canadian Social Trends* (Spring): 6–10. Statistics Canada Catalogue no. 11–008.

Tanner, Julian, Harvey Krahn, and Timothy F. Hartnagel. 1995. *Fractured Transitions from School to Work: Revisiting the Dropout Problem*. Toronto: Oxford University Press.

Taylor, Alison. 2000. *The Politics of Educational Reform in Alberta*. Toronto: University of Toronto Press.

Treaty 7 Elders and Tribal Council. 1996. *The True Spirit and Original Intent of Treaty 7*. Montreal and Kingston: McGill-Queen's University Press.

Trigger, Bruce G. 1985. *Natives and Newcomers: Canada's 'Heroic Age' Reconsidered*. Montreal and Kingston: McGill-Queen's University Press.

UN Working Group on Indigenous Populations. 1994. 'Draft Declaration on the Rights of Indigenous Peoples before the Working Group of Government', E/CN.4/Sub.2/1994/2/Add.1.

Voyageur, Cora J. 1996. 'Contemporary Indian Women', in D.A. Long and O.P. Dickason, eds, *Visions of the Heart: Canadian Aboriginal Issues*. Toronto: Harcourt Brace and Company, 93–115.

Wang, Margaret C., Geneva D. Haertl, and Herbert J. Walberg. 1998. *Building Educational Resilience*. Bloomington, Ind.: Phi Delta Kappan Educational Foundation.

West, W. Gordon. 1984. *Young Offenders and the State: A Canadian Perspective on Delinquency*. Toronto: Butterworths.

Wilson, Peggy. 1994. 'The Professor/Student Relationship: Key Factors in

Minority Student Performance and Achievement', *Canadian Journal of Native Studies* 14, 2: 305–17.

Working Margins Consulting Group. 1992. 'Indian Post-School Education in Saskatchewan'. Discussion Paper, prepared for the Office of the Treaty Commissioner, Saskatoon. Winnipeg: The Working Margins Consulting Group.

Wotherspoon, Terry. 1998. *The Sociology of Education in Canada: Critical Perspectives*. Toronto: Oxford University Press.

———. 2003. 'Aboriginal People, Public Policy and Social Differentiation in Canada', in Danielle Juteau, ed., *Social Differentiation: Patterns and Processes*. Toronto and Montreal: University of Toronto Press and University of Montreal Press.

——— and Joanne Butler. 1999. 'Informal Learning: Cultural Experiences and Entrepreneurship Among Aboriginal People', New Approaches to Lifelong Learning Working Paper Series 04–1999. Available at: <http://nall.oise.utoronto.ca>.

York, Geoffrey. 1992. *The Dispossessed: Life and Death in Native Canada*. Toronto: Little, Brown and Co.

INDEX

CPSIA information can be obtained at www.ICGtesting.com
Printed in the USA
LVOW090831250412

278972LV00007B/3/P